JIN YAN

MW00694361

Hong Kong University Press thanks Xu Bing for writing the Press's name in his Square Word Calligraphy for the covers of its books. For further information, see p. iv.

JIN YAN
The Rudolph Valentino of Shanghai

Richard J. Meyer

香港大學出版社
HONG KONG UNIVERSITY PRESS

Hong Kong University Press
14/F Hing Wai Centre
7 Tin Wan Praya Road
Aberdeen
Hong Kong

© Richard J. Meyer 2009

ISBN 978-962-209-586-1

All rights reserved. No portion of this publication may be reproduced or transmitted in any form or by any means, electronic or mechanical, including photocopy, recording, or any information storage or retrieval system, without permission in writing from the publisher.

Secure On-line Ordering
http://www.hkupress.org

British Library Cataloguing-in-Publication Data
A catalogue record for this book is available
from the British Library.

Printed and bound by ColorPrint Production Ltd., in Hong Kong, China

Hong Kong University Press is honoured that Xu Bing, whose art explores the complex themes of language across cultures, has written the Press's name in his Square Word Calligraphy. This signals our commitment to cross-cultural thinking and the distinctive nature of our English-language books published in China.

"At first glance, Square Word Calligraphy appears to be nothing more unusual than Chinese characters, but in fact it is a new way of rendering English words in the format of a square so they resemble Chinese characters. Chinese viewers expect to be able to read Square word Calligraphy but cannot. Western viewers, however are surprised to find they can read it. Delight erupts when meaning is unexpectedly revealed."

— Britta Erickson, *The Art of Xu Bing*

Contents

Illustrations

Photographs are courtesy of Qin Yi and the China Film Archive.

Photo 1   Jin Yan relaxes after a tennis match. He believed every actor should keep in excellent physical condition.

Photo 2   Jin often went horseback riding in the outskirts of Shanghai. He rode horses in several films.

Photo 3   Jin was an avid hunter and superb shot. He was comfortable using weapons in many of his films.

Photo 4   Jin was proficient in martial arts and swordplay. His first starring role was in *Feng Liu Jian Ke* (The Playboy Swordsman) directed by Sun Yu, 1929.

Photo 5   Jin Yan in his Hong Kong–tailored attire. The star was known for his sartorial splendor before the establishment of the PRC.

Photo 6   Jin had a reputation of late night drinking, smoking, and carousing.

Photo 7   Jin was happy when Mao Zedong established the PRC, but he never joined the Communist Party.

Photo 8   Jin's official photograph after he was chosen to be the head of the Actors' Guild by the CCP.

Foreword

Popular culture is a mirror on the political, economic, and social life of a nation. Richard Meyer's biography of Jin Yan is an excellent case in point.

As Meyer shows us, Jin was the Rudolph Valentino of his day, the 1930s–1950s, when China went through massive upheavals: the Japanese invasion and occupation of China, World War II, the dislocations caused not only by the war but famine and disease, and a ruthless Nationalist government that killed countless numbers of people to maintain its hold on power.

Jin was a movie star who not only entertained people, and by so doing distracted them from the travails of their daily lives, but also gained fame as an inspirational figure who gave people hope for a better day. His popularity was such that both the Nationalist and then the Communist governments gave him the freedom to make his films, which they did little to censor. Because Jin was able to mask most of his political antagonism to both regimes, he managed to survive or at least continue to make films that were seen by millions of people.

Yet in spite of his popularity, Jin, like so many millions of others in China, fell victim to the Cultural Revolution. He ended his years in relative obscurity as an invalid after some botched surgery.

Richard Meyer's biography rescues Jin from the shadows and brings him back to stage center in the China of the 1930s, 40s, and 50s. Jin's life is a vehicle for telling us about film in the China of these years, but also about the national temper. It is a story well worth telling and hearing.

Robert Dallek
January 2009

Preface

W hen writing my book about Ruan Ling-yu and screening all of her films, I kept coming across the actress's co-star Jin Yan. He appeared in many forms both on the screen and in her personal life. I could not help but admire him as he performed in her movies, but also as he continued to have an influence on her short and tragic life. Spending three whole days with Qin Yi, Jin's widow and a famous movie star, convinced me that his life was a story that needed to be told. Lai Shek arranged my introduction to her. There were no books about the actor in English or even Chinese. While Ruan remains an icon in China even today, Jin seemed to be invisible. He has been discovered recently in Korea, the land in which he was born, but from which he was forced to flee with his family as a small child.

Although Jin became a leading figure in China, he never forgot that he was a Korean. He assisted refugees from his native country providing funds for their school in Shanghai. In addition, he helped Korean filmmakers to secure jobs in China.

Thanks to the China Film Archive in Beijing, I was able to screen every film that still exists in which the actor appeared. As I viewed each motion picture, I realized why many of Jin's contemporaries referred to him as the "Chinese Valentino." Just as the Hollywood icon of the 1920s filled every frame in which he appeared, his Asian counterpart did exactly the same thing. The only other actor on the screen who showed this electricity with him was Ruan Ling-yu. The Archive also provided me with copies of the Encyclopedia of Chinese Films with information about his other films. Liu Dong and his staff cooperated with me literally day and night. Retired director Chen Jingliang assisted my efforts.

My fellowship in Dr. Peter Lehman's Center for Film, Media and Popular Culture at Arizona State University gave me the time to do important research. He and his colleagues were most kind in making available all of the resources at the institution.

The libraries at the University of Hawaii and the University of Washington were rich sources of material dealing with Chinese history and culture. Richard Carkeek at the East Asia Library at UW was extremely helpful in providing me with whatever I needed and Paula Walker gave me working space.

Friends in Hong Kong assisted me in discovering other ways to acquire more information about Jin Yan. Bede Cheng introduced me to Lai Shek and Ying Chan opened the doors again at Hong Kong University. Law Kar at the Hong Kong International Film Festival provided insights into the history of the period. My participation at the 100th Anniversary of Chinese Film Conference in Beijing enabled me to hear many presentations about early film production and to listen to Professor Cho Pock-rey's lecture about Jin Yan.

Dr. Yomi Braester, Associate Professor in Comparative Literature, Film Studies and East Asian Language and Literature at the University of Washington, provided me with many background materials which he published, as well as allowing me to view his collection of selected VCDs.

I could never have written my first book nor this one without my son Mahlon who speaks and writes Mandarin Chinese and who lived in China for many years. He translated the inter-titles of all of the films that I viewed at the archives. In addition, he sat long hours with me looking at DVDs and VCDs doing simultaneous translations of the sound dialogue. Mahlon also spent days interpreting the text of encyclopedic citations. Assisting me with translation were Xinyu Dong, Yang Wei and Chong Eun Ahn.

I have used the pinyin system of Romanization in the text except for the case of the well-known names and historical references.

My wife Susan Harmon encouraged me to tackle another book. My daughter Adina Carrick and my granddaughter Rowan helped with the typing. They were assisted by Michelle Cash, Matt Rogers, and Erin Baumgardt. My other daughter Rachel Meyer and my mother-in-law, Doris Harmon, supported my efforts.

Finally, I would like to thank Colin Day, Publisher of Hong Kong University Press, Michael Duckworth, Dawn Lau, and the staff, for giving me the opportunity to bring the story of Jin Yan from oblivion to the mainstream.

Richard J. Meyer
January 2009

Cast of Characters in the Life of Jin Yan

In order of appearance in the text

Deng Xiaoping — General Secretary of the Communist Party of China 1956–1967; chairman of the Central Military Commission of CCP 1981–1989; *de facto* leader of the People's Republic of China after Mao Zedong.

Rudolph Valentino — Hollywood leading man of the 1920s.

Wang Renmei — Jin Yan's first wife and Shanghai movie star.

Ruan Ling-yu — China's most famous silent motion picture actress who committed suicide at age twenty-four.

Mao Zedong — Chairman of the Communist Party of China (CCP) 1945–1976; president of the People's Republic of China 1954–1959.

Qin Yi — Jin Yan's second wife and famous Chinese film star.

King Kojung — King of Korea 1873–1905.

King Sun Jong — King of Korea 1905–1910.

Kim Pil Sun — Jin Yan's father.

Louis H. Severance — American philanthropist.

Kim Duck-lin — Jin Yan's name at birth.

Jin Xun — Jin Yan's middle-school name.

Zhou Enlai — Premier of the People's Republic of China 1949–1976; foreign minister of PRC 1949–1958.

Kim San — Anti-Japanese Korean activist and early member of the Korean Communist Party.

Kim Kyu Sik — Jin Yan's uncle.

Hou Yao — Writer and director at Minxin Film Company.

Li Minwei — Head of Minxin Film Company when he joined Luo Mingyou to form Lianhua.

Luo Mingyou — Owner and operator of movie theaters all over China in the 1920s and founder of Lianhua studios.

Sun Yu — U.S.-trained director who worked at Minxin and Lianhua.

Bu Wancang — Director at Mingxing film studios and later at Lianhua, lifelong friend of Jin Yan.

Chiang Kai-shek — President of the Republic of China 1928–1949; president of the Republic of China on Taiwan 1950–1975; leader of Guomindang (KMT).

Lu Xun — China's most famous writer of the twentieth century.

Tian Han — Revolutionary writer and director.

Zheng Zhengqin — Producer and director at Mingxing Studios.

Wan Laitian — Director and actor at Minxin Film Company.

Hu Die — The highest-paid movie star in Shanghai, known as "Butterfly Wu."

Fei Mu — Director and writer.

Chen Yanyan — One of the most famous actresses of the 1930s.

Cai Chusheng — Director at Lianhua and winner of China's first International Award for *Song of the Fishermen* at Moscow Film Festival.

Nie Er — Composer of many leftist songs and author of the official anthem of the People's Republic of China.

Li Lili — Actress at Lianhua.

Zhang Shankun — Founder of Xinhua Film Company.

Wu Yonggang — Director famous for his film *The Goddess*.

Zhang Zhizhi — Heavy-set actor who played villains at Lianhua.

Liu Qiong — Lifelong friend of Jin Yan and fellow basketball player and actor.

Wang Jingwei — Puppet president of China under Japanese occupation.

Kawakita Nagamasa — Head of all film production activities in Japanese-occupied Shanghai.

Ji Tienguo — Qin Yi's first husband.

Jin Jie — Son of Jin Yan and Qin Yi.

Jin Fei Hang — Jin Yan's step-daughter.

Jiang Qing — Wife of Mao Zedong, member of the "Gang of Four," in charge of all film activities during the Cultural Revolution.

Lin Biao — Head of the People's Liberation Army (PLA) during the Cultural Revolution.

Photo 1 Jin Yan relaxes after a tennis match. He believed every actor should keep in excellent physical condition.

Photo 2 Jin often went horseback riding in the outskirts of Shanghai. He rode horses in several films.

Photo 3 Jin was an avid hunter and superb shot. He was comfortable using weapons in many of his films.

Photo 4 Jin was proficient in martial arts and swordplay.
His first starring role was in *Feng Liu Jian Ke*
(The Playboy Swordsman) directed by Sun Yu, 1929.

Photo 5   Jin Yan in his Hong Kong–tailored attire. The star was known for his sartorial splendor before the establishment of the PRC.

Photo 6   Jin had a reputation of late night drinking, smoking, and carousing.

Photo 7 Jin was happy when Mao Zedong established the PRC,
but he never joined the Communist Party.

Photo 8 Jin's official photograph after he was chosen to be the head of the Actors' Guild by the CCP.

Photo 9 Jin was always studying. He learned English, German, and other languages by himself. The actor reviewed all film scripts and made revisions to make the characters he was playing appear realistic.

Photo 10 Jin spent time knitting when he was not acting. He designed a sweater in which the sleeves covered his hands but the writing fingers were exposed for use in cold weather.

Photo 11 Jin had a talent for carving and possessed an imported tool kit which he hid from the Red Guards during the Cultural Revolution.

Photo 12 When Jin became ill and had to spend all his days at home, he became proficient in drawing which he studied at Nankai. Several artists visited him and admired his talent.

Photo 13 Jin Yan and Ruan Ling-yu in their first film together *Yecao Xianhua* (Wild Flower), 1930. The pair became a sensation and Shanghai movie fans clamored for more. The story was about class struggle. In one scene, Jin as Huang Yu, teaches Ruan, who plays Lilian, to master a musical instrument.

Photo 14 Jin as a famous movie star in the film within a film *Yin Han Shuang Xing* (Two Stars Shining in the Milky Way), 1931. The "Milky Way" was a popular Chinese term for "silver screen."

Photo 15 Jin Yan, as De'en, the landowner's son with
Ruan Ling-yu as the innocent peasant in *Taohua Qi Xue Ji*
(The Peach Girl), 1931, in a story about the evils of feudalism.

Photo 16 Jin, the wealthy landlord's son, invites Ruan,
who plays the naïve maiden, to visit him in the city where
he seduces her in *Taohua Qi Xue Ji* (The Peach Girl), 1931.

Photo 17 Wang Renmei, Jin's first wife, was discovered by director Sun Yu, when she acted and sang with the Bright Moon Choir.

Photo 18 Jin as Jiang Bo, a wealthy painter, and his friend from the slums played by Zheng Junli in *Ye Meigui* (Wild Rose), 1932. They join the volunteers to fight the invaders of China.

Photo 19 Wang Renmei in her first film as Little Wind in *Ye Meigui* (Wild Rose), 1932. Jin started an affair with the young actress during the filming.

Photo 20 Wang Renmei, directed by Sun Yu and coached by Jin, soon was known in the press as "Wild Rose." She married Jin in 1934.

Photo 21 Jin Yan as Jia Hu, breaking rocks in the quarry in
Mu Xing Zhi Guang (Maternal Radiance), 1931.
Director Bu Wancang became one of Jin's lifelong friends.

Photo 22 Jin, bare-chested as usual, works with his team of fellow road
builders in *Da Lu* (The Big Road) directed by Sun Yu, 1934. In a later
scene, the actor and his buddies remove their clothes to go swimming.

Photo 23 Jin appeared with Wang Renmei in a stage play
The Song for a Returning Spring, written by Tian Han. The author
was hiding from the KMT police who later arrested him.

Photo 24 Jin plays Shun Er who leads the peasants in their fight against
bandits in *Zuang Zhi Ling Yun* (Soaring Aspirations), 1936.

Photo 25 The wedding photo of Jin Yan and Qin Yi. They were married in Hong Kong in 1947. It was the second marriage for both of them.

Photo 26 Jin is Situ Yan, an investigative journalist, in *Sheng Long Kuai Xu* (Riding the Dragon), 1948. He survives a beating by gangsters to continue his work in another city.

Photo 27 Jin Yan and Qin Yi greet their fans. Qin went on to become one of the most popular actresses in China while Jin had trouble securing roles after the establishment of the PRC.

Photo 28 Qin Yi holds their son Jin Jie as the proud father admires the boy. Later, Jin's son developed mental problems.

Photo 29 Jin and Qin with Jin Jie and the actress's daughter from her first marriage, Jin Fei Heng.

Photo 30 Qin and Jin were crazy about their son. Although Jin Jie was retarded, his father taught him to play ping pong and other sports.

Photo 31 Jin and Qin only appeared together in one film,
Shiqu De Aiqing (Lost Love), 1949. Moviegoers were elated
that the pair would unite on the screen as they had done in real life.

Photo 32 Qin plays Qiu Li Yin and Jin is Qin Fang Qian in
Shiqu De Aiqing (Lost Love), 1949. The heroine dies at
the end before she can be reunited with her lover.

Photo 33 Qin Yi and Jin Yan realize that her husband in the film is a traitor and is a spy for the Japanese in *Shiqu De Aiqing* (Lost Love), 1949. The film was released after the Communists seized Shanghai.

Photo 34 Jin Yan and Jin Jie just before the establishment of the PRC. Jin still dressed in his Hong Kong–tailored Western-style clothes.

Photo 35 Qin Yi and Jin Yan with their son after the CCP takeover. Their clothes changed to fit the times.

Photo 36 Jin as Old Shen in *Da Di Chong Guang* (The Return of Spring), 1950. The actor's part as a machine-gunner provided him with the opportunity to demonstrate his cooperation with the new studio leaders.

Photo 37 Jin was happy at first as head of the Actors' Guild.
He treated Qin's daughter as his own and she helped take care of
her step-brother and her niece when their parents were working.

Photo 38 Qin and Jin were
pleased with the work of the
Shanghai Film Company which
they helped establish after
liberation. Later, Yan'an cadres
exerted their influence.

Photo 39 Jin Yan signs autographs in Beijing after winning the model worker award. He and his wife were delighted with the honor.

Photo 40 Jin accepts his prize given by the Communist Party in 1951. He wrote Qin the first and only letter of their relationship. She felt a new sense of intimacy again. That was to change when the actress discovered Jin's infidelity.

Photo 41 Jin is Old Deng, a 1930s Communist leader,
in *Mu Qin* (Mother), 1956. Although his character is executed in the
middle of the film, Jin assisted Zhang Ruifang, who stars as
the mother, with her acting technique.

Photo 42 Jin plays Lao Ba'er, the Tibetan hunter in *Bao Feng Yu Zhong
De Xiong Ying* (Eagles Brave before the Storm), 1957. The film was shot
in Tibet and conditions on location were horrible.

Photo 43 Jin is Party Secretary Tang in *Hai Shang Hong Qi*
(Red Flag over the Sea), 1958. The actor brought his naturalistic style
to the role and refused to become a cardboard character.

Photo 44 Jin's last film *Ai Chang Ru Jia* (Love the Factory as Your
Home), 1958, is a good example of the Great Leap Forward genre.
The actor plays the district industry director who encourages
the workers to establish higher goals of production.

Photo 46 Qin is congratulated by Zhou Enlai for her many screen roles. The premier of the PRC was a great supporter of the film industry and tried to help them during the Cultural Revolution.

Photo 45 When Jin no longer appeared in films, he helped Qin Yi with her roles and encouraged her to seek leading parts. He listened to her singing and gave constructive criticisms.

Photo 47 Qin and Jin just before they were sent away during the Cultural Revolution. The actor was exiled from Shanghai for one year while his wife was away for four.

Photo 48 When Deng Xiaoping returned to power after the death of Mao, China became more open and instituted a modified capitalism. Here Qin Yi shows visiting American movie star Gregory Peck her native city of Shanghai.

Photo 49 The author Richard J. Meyer with Jin Fei Hang, Qin Yi and Jin Jie in Shanghai. He spent three days interviewing Qin.

CHAPTER 1

Growing Up in Exile

W hen the State Administration of Radio, Film and TV opened its beautiful National Film Museum to celebrate the 100th anniversary of Chinese film in 2005, the most famous leading man of the pre-Communist era was resurrected from obscurity. There in the main gallery depicting the history of Chinese film was the portrait of Jin Yan with scenes from his most famous motion pictures. Why, after being erased from memory during the Cultural Revolution, did the so-called "Emperor of Film" re-emerge in this massive, modern glass and steel structure,[1] an edifice described by *The New York Times* as "spectacular"?[2]

Jin Yan's life spanned the most turbulent period in modern Chinese history. Born in Korea during the Japanese occupation, he was taken as a child to China for safety. His story through the years enabled him to survive under the corrupt Republican government of the Guomindang (KMT), the Japanese aggression against Shanghai, World War II, the Chinese Civil War, the victory of the Communists (CCP), the Cultural Revolution and the beginning of Deng Xiaoping's economic reforms.

Jin accomplished his greatest stardom during the 1930s. He was often compared with Rudolph Valentino in the way he dominated each frame he was in. Women literally threw themselves at his feet. Married at first to fellow star Wang Renmei, he enjoyed his status as an icon. His movie role with Ruan Ling-yu, the icon of her time, had the public demanding more of them together. It was Jin who made Ruan, the screen goddess, aware of the potential of film to portray the social ills of the time and yet evade the KMT censors with melodramatic soap opera formats.

Jin's embodiment of the May Fourth[3] ideals of the time, through his sensual and raw appearances in the most popular films, added a new layer of sexuality to the liberal movement, a persona that the Communists initially accepted. Later, it was rejected in their campaign to "learn from Lei Feng," when Mao Zedong used the suffering and altruism of this young soldier who died in the service of the people as an example for the youth of China. The new heroes of the People's Republic such as Lei Feng, though robust, marked a massive turnabout from the raw sexuality and reign of Jin Yan at his height. And, as Qin Yi, Jin's second wife, rose to new heights as a film star in a politically charged world of cadre movie actors, the aging performer, sick and convalescent, was allowed to languish in obscurity. Although he appeared in thirty-nine films, mostly as the star, his death was hardly noticed except by his family and a very few faithful friends.

To understand what shaped the life of Jin Yan and why he was forgotten, one must examine the turmoil of the twentieth century in China and especially the role of Japanese aggression on the Korean and Chinese population. The two nations that border one another on the Asian continent have had a symbiotic relationship for centuries.

Korea had been traditionally under Chinese influence for hundreds of years paying substantial tribute to the Ming dynasty during the *Pax Sinica*.[4] When the Japanese invaded Korea in the sixteenth century, Ming troops came to the aid of their "little brother" and forced the aggressors to observe a truce. Korea was devastated as 200,000 Japanese and 222,000 Chinese soldiers fought on the peninsula. Many of the survivors of the battles remained and married native women while some Koreans journeyed to China and Japan.[5] The Ming court, weakened by its war against Japan, was overthrown by the Manchus in 1644. The new dynasty invaded Korea to secure a pledge of loyalty from the Korean monarch which was done. "Koreans felt a moral obligation toward their 'elder brother'." This type of tributary diplomacy continued under the Qing dynasty as well.[6]

China, however, in the latter half of the nineteenth century, weakened by the massive Taiping rebellion and the Opium War, was not able to protect its "little brother." Japan, seeking to open Korea to its commerce, sent a warship to the peninsula in 1875. The vessel received cannon fire from the shore whereupon the Japanese landed, killed many Korean soldiers, looted villages and captured weapons and gunpowder. The Chosen court was forced to sign the Kanghua Treaty which opened Korea to Japanese interests.[7]

In 1882, a group of Korean nationalists attacked the Japanese legation in Seoul and murdered one of its military advisors.[8] Both China and Japan sent troops to keep the peace. The common expression at that time was that Korea had become "a shrimp between two whales."[9] During the Sino-Japanese War in 1895, a peasant uprising on the peninsula was crushed by the Japanese. When the Qing was defeated it was forced to sign the Treaty of Shimonoseki in which it recognized Korea as an independent kingdom and not as a tributary of China. As Russia attempted to exert influence over Korea, the Russo-Japanese War ensued in 1904 with a quick defeat for the Czarist nation. The Treaty of Portsmouth the next year provided for Japan's authority over Korea.

In November 1905, Japanese troops occupied Seoul and declared Korea a protectorate.[10]

The occupiers forced King Kojong to abdicate and placed his son Crown Prince Sunjong on the throne. His first act was to sign a revised treaty which placed Japanese as deputy ministers at all of the government ministries. This procedure was the real beginning of strong anti-Japanese sentiments among the Korean people.[11]

At this time, Kim Pil Sun graduated from the prestigious Severance Hospital Medical School which was started in Seoul by Presbyterian missionaries and funded by American philanthropist Louis H. Severance.[12] The young doctor almost immediately became involved with the anti-Japanese movement. The occupying army had started a vast military campaign against the resistance. In 1908, for example, the Japanese army killed 12,000 members of the Korean underground guerrillas. When Japanese sympathizers were assassinated, two Imperial Army Divisions occupied Korea, "making the nation virtually a police state." On August 22, 1910, Japan formally annexed the country which eliminated the protectorate and ended the Chosen dynasty.[13] Yet, between 1906 and 1914, there was a continued armed insurgency against the Japanese in Korea.[14]

The thirty-five years of Japanese colonial rule over Korea has been referred to as three periods. The first (military rule) was annexation from 1910 to the 1919 March First Movement,[15] the second (cultural politics) occurred from 1919 to the Japanese takeover of Manchuria in 1931, and the third (fascist system) lasted from 1931 to Japan's defeat in World War II in 1945.[16]

By 1911, all political activities were prohibited and Koreans could not exercise freedom of speech, press and assembly. Furthermore, they were "discouraged" from attending college and "encouraged" to learn the Japanese language. One year later, the occupying forces instituted savage interrogation methods and punishments such as flogging.[17] It was then that Dr. Kim Pul Sun, by now a prominent and well-to-do surgeon, decided to flee with his entire family including five sons, two daughters, his wife and his aged mother. One of his sons, two-year-old Kim Duck-lin, was destined to one day be one of the most famous screen stars in pre–World War II China. His exile had begun.[18]

As the Kim family crossed the Yalu River, they turned their heads back toward the country most of them would never see again. Thousands of Koreans had preceded them and had settled in Manchuria. Some even had escaped in large numbers to Shanghai where they established a Provisional Government of the Republic of Korea in 1919.[19] Others carried out hit-and-run attacks on Japanese troops from the border areas of China. When the Japanese invaded Manchuria in 1931, they retaliated by killing innocent Korean civilians.[20]

Dr. Kim moved at first to Tonghua in northern Manchuria and then about a year later in 1913 the family settled in Qiqihaer in Heilongjiang Province. His son, Duck-lin, learned about the Japanese conquest and their atrocities from his father who continued his support for the ouster of the Japanese from Korea. In 1919, Kim died. The nine-year-old boy learned that his father's illness and death were caused by the enemies of his country. Some say Dr. Kim was assassinated. The youngster and his family scattered to different cities in China as his mother realized they would not be safe so close to the border. He was sent to an aunt, his father's sister, in Shanghai, where he was an exceptional student and learned to speak Mandarin without a trace of an accent. It was there in that sophisticated city that he saw his first film, *Tian Nü San Hua*, and decided he would become a movie star.[21]

Jin Yan was captivated when he spent that afternoon in the theater watching Mei Lanfang, the greatest opera star in Chinese history, on the screen. Mei also directed the film which was based on the traditional Peking Opera drama "Heavenly Fairy Tossing Flowers." The actor/director played the heavenly fairy who is asked by Buddha to drop flowers on a sick monk and toss petals on his disciples.[22]

It must have seemed that here was the answer for the death of his father: A beautiful fairy with the ineffable power to cure. The movie must have seemed almost an alternate life where his father would never have to die.

Duck-lin had to move again when he was thirteen. He stayed with his older brother in Jinan, Shandong, for a short time and then returned to live with his aunt whose husband had just been appointed Professor at Beiyang University in Tianjin. The boy demonstrated a strong independent spirit and did various odd jobs at school to earn money for his living expenses.

From 1925 to 1927, while attending Nankai Middle-High School (Zhou Enlai's alma mater as well), he was influenced by the May Fourth writers, especially Lu Xun, China's most famous twentieth-century author. He changed his name to Jin Xun, then soon afterward to Jin Yan, who had been the hero of one of Lu's novels. From then on Jin Yan became his stage and screen name.[23] He had already entered, in name at least, into a world that defied death and suffering with romantic resistance.

Another enormous influence on the adolescent Jin was meeting twenty-year-old anti-Japanese activist Kim San, considered one of the heroes of the Korean Independence Movement. Many called him the "Che Guevara of the East."[24] He, like many of the one million Korean exiles in China, never forgot how the Japanese government used the language of international diplomacy to justify their takeover of Korea. The conquering nation's strategy was to create "a perception among the nations of the 'civilized' world that Japan was *the* modern, legal nation in Asia."[25] They also remembered the 1905 deal between the United States and Japan which recognized the American interest in the Philippines and Japanese suzerainty over Korea. In the same year, Japan "traded India for Korea" with Great Britain.[26]

Kim San told Jin about his journey from Korea in 1919 and his study of military science in Manchuria. From there, the young man joined "the little knot of Korean revolutionaries" in Shanghai.[27] The revolutionary taught the eager listener the Korean folk song which had been recited by countless exiles and was banned by the Japanese. The sorrow mixed with its martial air became part of Jin's personality. Even on screen his persona seemed to reflect the spirit of the song that would become his personal creed: a rare mix of hidden sorrow and masculinity.

> Ariran, Ariran, Arari O!
> Crossing the hills of Ariran.
> There are twelve hills of Ariran
> And now I am crossing the last hill.
>
> Many stars in the deep sky —
> Many crimes in the life of man.
> Ariran, Ariran, Arari O!
> Crossing the hills of Ariran.
>
> Ariran is the mountain of sorrow
> And the path to Ariran has no returning.
> Ariran, Ariran, Arari O!
> Crossing the hills of Ariran.
>
> Oh, twenty million countrymen —
>   where are you now?
> Alive are only three thousand *li*
>   of mountains and rivers.
> Ariran, Ariran, Arari O!
> Crossing the hills of Ariran.

> Now I am an exile crossing the Yalu River
> And the mountains and rivers of three thousand
>   *li* are also lost.
> Ariran, Ariran, Arari O!
> Crossing the hills of Ariran.[28]

Before graduation, with money he had saved from his many school-related jobs, he told his uncle Kim Kyu Sik that he wanted to go to Shanghai to become an actor. He was met with strong objection from the Professor and Korean independence advocate. Jin stayed at Nankai for a little while longer starring on the school's basketball team. When the athlete confided in his teammates that he did not have enough for the fare, they chipped in and provided him with the opportunity to travel to the "Paris of Asia" to seek either ruin or fame.[29] But he never forgot his friendship with Kim San nor the lessons he learned from his father. The memory of his childhood and the struggles of the Korean people against their Japanese overlords were to influence him and his career for the rest of his life. Now thinking only of the silver screen, he boarded the ship to Shanghai and imagined his new life to come.

Notes

1. *The International Herald Tribune*, January 26, 2006.
2. *The New York Times*, April 1, 2007.
3. John King Fairbank, *China: A New History* (Cambridge, MA and London, England: The Belknap Press of Harvard University Press, 1992), pp. 267–8. Urban protests on May 4, 1919 against the Treaty of Versailles's award to Japan of former German-held territory gave rise to the movement know as "The May Fourth Movement." The movement led by intellectuals brought new cultural ideas of science and democracy and patriotism into an anti-imperialist agenda. Literature written in the vernacular was the most popular way to spread its message. Later, film became the medium that reached a wider audience. See also Chow Tse-

tsung, *The May Fourth Movement* (Cambridge, MA: Harvard University Press, 1960).

4. Jun Kil Kim, *The History of Korea* (Westport, CN: Greenwood Press, 2005), pp. 74–8.
5. Ibid., pp. 80–4.
6. Ibid., pp. 85–6.
7. Ibid., pp. 104–7.
8. *The Encyclopedia of World History*, http://www.bartleby.com/67/1430. html.
9. Kim, op. cit., p. 108.
10. Ibid., pp. 111–21.
11. Ibid., pp. 123–4.
12. As the number of graduates increased, the faculty of the school at first consisted of missionary doctors. They were gradually replaced by its own graduates. The school remained the only medical school operating for Koreans by Koreans until the end of the Japanese occupation. It is now called the Yonsei University College of Medicine. http://medicine. yonsei.ac.kr/en.
13. Kim, op. cit., p. 125.
14. Alexis Dudden, *Japan's Colonization of Korea: Discourse and Power* (Honolulu: University of Hawaii Press, 2005), p. 76.
15. The March First Movement started with the reading of the Korean Declaration of Independence on March 1, 1919 by a group of nationalists in Seoul and was influenced by U.S. President Woodrow Wilson's "Fourteen Points" of self-determination. Massive crowds assembled and were massacred by the Japanese. 7,500 were killed, 16,000 wounded and 47,000 arrested.
16. Mau-Gil Kang, *A History of Contemporary Korea* (Folkestone, U.K.: Global Oriental, 2005), pp. 3–4.
17. Kim, op. cit., p. 126.
18. Cho Pock-rey, *Blooming Flower in Shanghai: The Emperor of Shanghai Movies of the 1930s, Jin Yan* (Seoul: Juluesung Press, 2004), p. 19.
19. Ibid., p. 132.
20. Kang, op. cit., pp. 38–9.
21. Cho Pock-rey, "The Emperor of Shanghai Movies of the 1930s, Jin Yan," *Asian Cinema*, Fall/Winter, 2003, p. 206.

22. *Encyclopedia of Chinese Films,* Vol. 1 (Beijing: China Movie Publishing House, 1996), p. 9.
23. Cho, *Blooming Flower in Shanghai*, pp. 43–5.
24. *The Korea Times*, August 15, 2005.
25. Dudden, pp. 28–9.
26. Ibid., pp. 62–3.
27. Nym Wales (Helen Foster Snow) and Kim San, *Song of Ariran: A Korean Communist in the Chinese Revolution* (San Francisco: Ramparts Press, 1941), p. 57.
28. Ibid., p. 56.
29. Cho, *Blooming Flower in Shanghai*, pp. 43–5.

CHAPTER 2

Breaking into the Shanghai Film World

The old steamer headed up-current just before dawn on March 8, 1927. The filthy waters of the Huangpu River splashed against its hull as it passed Japanese, British, and American warships anchored in mid-channel. A tall seventeen-year-old man clung to the railing of the vessel as it pushed aside junks laden with food, lumber, and other goods from the interior of China. The boy could smell the fetid odors of the thousands of souls who inhabited small sampans and shacks along the banks. He scarcely noticed the corpses floating on the surface. All he could think about was that at last he was here at Shanghai, the "Hollywood of Asia."

Jin Yan spied the art deco buildings on the Bund and heard the clock on the Customs Tower strike six. The sun was rising and so were his spirits. The "Paris of Asia" was familiar to Jin as he had lived in Shanghai when he was thirteen. Even though his friend Kim San had advised him to visit the Korean People's Association first, he made his way to the offices of the Minxin Film Company (China Sun Film Company). Jin introduced himself to Hou Yao, the writer and director of one of Shanghai's biggest hits of 1927, *The Romance of the Western Chamber*. The young man made a good impression and was hired to copy scripts and take notes. Hou even arranged for the newcomer to perform as an extra. The director also secured accommodations for him. So with seven renminbi to his name, he was able to support himself and learn about the movie business. His mentor had written a book about the importance of writing screenplays. Hou stated in *How to Write a Script for an Electric Shadowplay* that, "Film script is the soul of film."[1] The director introduced Jin to the work of Ibsen and his view "art for life's sake." Hou taught his apprentice that film should educate society and deal with social problems.

Following in the trend, the Minxin Film Company was started by Chinese film pioneer Li Minwei who later was to form Lianhua (United Film Company) with Luo Mingyou in 1930. Li had hired rising stars in film directing and screenwriting for Minxin such as Bu Wancang and Sun Yu. They also became part of the great Lianhua studios in the 1930s.[2] Jin's destiny would be linked forever with the film company.

The young man's first month in Shanghai was not only an education in film but in raw politics. Strikes had been paralyzing the city off and on for months. In Nanjing, the British, American, and Japanese consulates were attacked, which prompted quick reprisal by a naval bombardment by British and American ships. Chiang Kai-shek, after success leading the Northern Expedition to quell rebellious warlords, was welcomed as he entered Shanghai.[3] The KMT leader, in a surprise move, after a few weeks in the city, ordered his troops, supported by the gangsters (notably the Green Gang) of the metropolis to slaughter all members of the CCP and their sympathizers. His actions were supported by both the Shanghai business and merchant classes, who feared the disruptive effects of militant labor activity and the foreign powers, who favored a quick return to normality.[4] The Japanese especially supported Chiang in

1927 because of his anti-Communist action as well as his purging of radical KMT members.[5] It is no surprise that the generalissimo decided to appease Japan in their attempt to conquer China. His overall strategy was to annihilate the Communists completely, unify the country under the KMT banner and then negotiate with the Japanese.

On the surface, it appeared as if Shanghai was free of all Communist Party members. While thousands were killed, hundreds went underground or fled to the countryside. The most successful film studio of the 1920s, Mingxing (Star Film Company), was infiltrated by the CCP.[6] Left-wing sympathizers and May Fourth writers continued to influence the other film production houses as well.

In November, Jin Yan lost his job at the Minxin studios. He began to write a novel inspired by his hero Lu Xun. To support himself, he worked part-time for a real estate agency showing rooms to prospective clients. In exchange, he received a place to sleep, but no salary. Each day, the lad ate two bowls of Yangchun noodles at a tiny noodle shop in the back alley. He asked the owner if he could charge the tab and he would pay when he got a job at another film studio. Every day Jin had his two bowls of noodles. Finally, the proprietor requested payment. Without funds, the young man took off his overcoat and gave it to the owner. Just like Oliver Twist, Jin then asked for more noodles on credit.[7]

While writing his book, Jin started to attend gatherings at the Southern China Society. The group consisted of artists and authors who were followers of the May Fourth movement and had vigorous anti-imperialistic and anti-feudalistic views. Many were underground Communists. The leader of the Society was playwright and left-wing activist Tian Han. It was he who became Jin's second mentor and the most important political influence of his life.[8] Tian became Jin's "older brother" and remained one of his best friends until he died. The first day of their meeting in the courtyard of the Society's building in Shanghai was implanted in Jin's memory. The great writer came running down the stairs to shake the young man's hand and welcome him to the organization. A few years later, when Tian's house was destroyed by Japanese bombs in 1932, the writer moved in with Jin Yan, who by this time had achieved stardom.[9]

Tian Han was directing one of his plays in early 1928 when the lead actor failed to show up. Then came Jin's big break. He asked Jin to step in at the last minute and play the male protagonist, a role Jin had observed during many rehearsals. That was the beginning of his acting career both on the stage and on film.[10] Yet Jin made his own success.

He kept leaving his resumés at various film studios. They were written in handsome characters, almost calligraphy. He finally secured a position as a ticket taker at a local cinema. At least, he thought, he could see films for free as well as being one step away from the other side of the screen. A lucky break for Jin occurred when director Zheng Qin of the Mingxing Film Company happened to see the resume. The director was impressed with the artistic nature of his handwriting and contacted Jin to serve as a recording secretary for writers at Mingxing. The job was to listen to them talk through a screen scenario and write it down for the actors.[11] Now Jin had another veteran from whom to learn about cinema. Zheng was a sophisticated screenwriter and director. He believed that film was an entertainment product as one category of drama and yet it had a social responsibility to inform and serve a purpose. He stated, "A play of supreme quality must contain the vitality of creating life. Second, it should also include the properties to criticize the society. To make things simpler, it should pick faults of social affairs for criticism so as to help the audience understand the error of the matter involved."[12] Many of his films were critical of the social system of feudalism, arranged marriage, and the subjugation of women. However, they were designed to appeal to a mass audience and were criticized as "mild with idealistic colors."[13]

Yet, as useful as the apprentice was to Zhang, his job did not call for acting. Jin kept searching and was able to secure a bit part, back at Minxin, as a soldier in *Mu Lan Cong Jun* (Hua Mulan Joins the Army), directed by his old mentor Hou Yao. The film was a huge box-office success and was based on the great Chinese folk tale of the girl who disguises herself as a man and leads the Chinese army to victory over the invading forces. Walt Disney loved this story so much he made it into an animated feature film in 1998. Both cinema versions have happy endings when Mulan takes off her male battle costume, becomes a female again, and gets the man she loves.

Jin's athletic build as a soldier in *Hua Mulan Joins the Army* was noticed by Wan Laitian who directed and acted in Minxin's first film of 1929, *Rexue Nan'er* (The Hot-Blooded Man). He selected the nineteen-year-old to play the role of the blacksmith.[14] The story is about Uncle Zhang, an old miser played by Wan who, with his young son, operate a cart for hire. Zhang wants to marry the iron forger's teenage daughter but cannot afford the wedding ceremony. After ten years of saving money, he is about to claim the girl but his son, by now a grown man, steals the money and gives it to support the defense of the country. The father is upset but later the son rescues a rich female student from bandits. She arranges jobs at her home for the two of them. After being mistaken for an intruder in the girl's room, the boy is fired by her father. When the wealthy father tries to force his daughter to marry an older man for money, she asks Zhang to help her escape in his cart. The final scene has both father and son pushing the girl in their cart on the road away from her home.[15]

While Jin's part was small and came only at the beginning of *The Hot-Blooded Man*, he caught the eye of Sun Yu who had just joined Minxin after making two films in 1928 for the Changcheng Film Company. Sun was hired to write and direct *Feng Liu Jian Ke* (Playboy Swordman). The American-trained director was looking for a handsome swashbuckling individual with good athletic skills. The script called for the hero to rescue a beautiful damsel on a runaway horse. Sun saw a photo of Jin as a blacksmith with muscles bulging. He then made inquires about the young man's work ethic at the studio. When Sun met Jin for the first time, he found him to be, "handsome and strong looking like a new type of student," according to Wang Renmei who believed that type of student embodied modernization and westernization and a new lifestyle.[16]

During the interview, Sun told Jin about his background to ease the tension. He explained that he had attended Nankai Middle and High School in Tianjin. After graduating from Qinghua University with a degree in literature he received a grant to study in the United States on a Boxer Indemnity Fund scholarship. At the University of Wisconsin, he translated the works of eighth-century poet Li Po. Sun was an honor graduate and his writing was praised by the faculty. He then went to New York City, studied at the New York Institute of Photography, attended a theater school run by American dramatist David Belasco, and enrolled at Columbia University for its night classes in film.

Acquiring the skills that later would lead the press to call him "the poet of film," Sun learned about photography, film processing, editing, acting, make-up, script writing, and directing in that one year in New York. He further enhanced his education by traveling extensively in Britain, France, Italy, and the Soviet Union before boarding the Trans-Siberian Express back to his home in China.[17]

Jin was relieved to hear about the Nankai school connection and told the director about how its basketball team had pooled money for his passage to Shanghai. He was eager to prove that he had the talent for the lead role in the film, especially because the story had sword fights and martial arts. Both men expressed their patriotic spirit and may have discussed how the May Thirtieth Movement led to the rise of Chinese martial arts films produced by the hundreds at all of the studios.[18]

Sun described the plot to Jin and told him he would play Long Fei, the lead. In the story, Long goes to greet his distant cousin Lu Xiaoxia, played by Gao Qianping, who admires a wild rose growing by a cliff. Long immediately picks it up for her and hands it to her, while she is mounted on her horse. Soon after, a servant who is accompanying the girl falls off his horse after going to sleep. The thud frightens Lu's horse and it becomes a runaway. Long chases after her, grabs the reins and saves Lu. Later at a county tavern, Lu laughs as two swordsmen, Bai Qi and Niu Zhengfeng are surrounded by singing wenches asking them for tips. She drops her rose carelessly and Long picks it up from the floor realizing he is infatuated with her. Bai glances at Lu and is stunned by her beauty. Later, the swordsmen and Long become acquainted at the bar and vow to be friends. The next day, bandits attack Long as he and Lu are journeying to his mansion. At first, Long's martial arts skills hold off the bandits, but there are too many of them. Just as it looks bad for the hero, Niu and Bai come to the rescue and the bandits flee. Long invites them to his home where they practice martial arts together and perform the ritual, which recognizes one another as brothers.

Long does not realize that Bai and Lu have fallen in love. One day, he tries to express his love in ambiguous language. Lu thinks that he is telling her Bai's intention to propose marriage. Their intimate conversation is seen but not heard by Bai, who thinks Lu is cheating on him. He insults both publicly. Long knocks him down and asks for an apology whereupon Bai challenges Long to a duel. The latter has much better skills, but wants to die because he knows Lu does not love him, and allows Bai to thrust at him resulting in a wound to his arm. Bai refuses to fight any longer when he remembers his vow of brotherly love. When Lu becomes angry at Bai's behavior, Long asks her not to end her relationship with Bai. Later, bandits surround the mansion and Long asks Bai to guard the house and he will fight them outside. After many martial arts scenes, including *Qigong*, Long is stabbed by the bandit leader and passes out. Bai comes outside and finds the fatally wounded Long and fights the bandits alone. He comes across the leader and stabs him at the throat. The rest of the villains run away. As he lay dying, Long tells Lu to marry Bai. When she nods, he dies with a smile on his face.[19]

The film, while not commercially successful, did display Jin's talents. The public was tired of these old knight errant pot-boilers. However, two critics in a spirit of anti-imperialism liked its message. "The nature of the Chinese nation sometimes seems one that is cowardly and content with temporary ease and comfort, not daring to raise its head and fight against the oppressors. What *Feng Liu Jian Ke* expresses … is a real reflection of the true revolutionary spirit."[20] Another said, "The rebellious spirit and indomitable courage is exactly what the Chinese urgently and presently ought to have."[21] According to Hu Jubin, martial arts films "stressed the imaginary element of superhuman strength in martial arts, which reflected Chinese audiences' introspection about their physical and mental weakness and their spiritual resistance to the resulting Western designation, 'The Sick Man of Asia (*Dongya Bingfu*)'."[22]

Both Sun and Jin, while pleased with the technical aspects of their latest production, were disheartened by its box-office failure.

In fact, most Shanghai-produced films were having trouble because they could not compete with American and European imports. Suddenly, things began to change when Hollywood sound movies were introduced. The Chinese audiences did not understand the language. In the silent era, few inter-titles were needed and these were translated into Chinese characters which could be understood all over the country, whatever the language spoken.

The staff at Minxin soon learned that Luo Mingyou had established a new film company and called it Lianhua (United China Film Company). Luo had persuaded their studio boss, Li Minwei, to join Da Zhonghua-Baihe, Shanghai Motion Pictures, and Hong Kong Film Companies to merge into this new enterprise.

Luo had years of experience operating movie theaters all over China and saw that American imports had been responsible for the bulk of the audience. Chinese films with their low budgets and poor production, in comparison, could not compete. He realized that with the distribution of Hollywood sound features in 1929, he had a chance to salvage the Shanghai film studio. When he realized that the foreign producers were not making any more silent films, Luo decided to continue that mode with his new company for several more years. Silent films could continue to be a universal language for Chinese. But he needed a partner.

Li Minwei, often referred to as the father of Chinese film, agreed with him. He started in cinema in 1913 in Hong Kong but made his reputation by filming the inauguration of President Sun Yat-sen in 1924.[23] Both he and Luo acknowledged to produce Chinese films of high quality for the domestic market, employing the best directors, writers, and actors in the country. Lianhua emerged in early 1930.[24]

The purpose of Lianhua was to revitalize national films by popularizing social education and to reform the old pot-boiler themes which focused on popular superstitions, bloody action sequences, and old-fashioned martial arts.[25]

Sun was delighted with the news. Now he would have a stable of the most talented writers, actors, set designers, and cinematographers from all over China. Li informed Sun that he would direct Lianhua's first film, which began as a co-production between Li's and Luo's two companies. Scriptwriter Zhu Shilin was hired to write *Gudu Chunmeng* (Memories of the Old Capital/Spring Dream in the Old Capital), which takes place in old Beijing. Sun was selected because there were plans to shoot on location in the ancient capital. The U.S.-trained director had the experience to handle a crew away from Shanghai. In addition, it was thought that he could have a positive influence on a rising star that had come from the Dazhonghua-Baihe Film Company. Ruan Ling-yu, who later became the most popular screen icon in 1930s China, became a more sophisticated actress under the guidance of Sun's direction.[26]

At first, Jin was apprehensive, but he was reassured by Sun that he was planning to make another film with Ruan and Jin would be her co-star. He gave the young actor a draft of the script, which he had written and told Jin that he would shoot the outdoor scenes, while he was in Beijing filming *Gudu Chenmeng*. The crew had to wait for almost the entire month of January 1930 for it to snow, and while they were there produced another film, *Zisha Hetong* (Suicide Contract).

When Sun and the crew returned to Shanghai in February, they had to shoot the interior scenes for both of the films. The director suddenly became ill and Jin wondered if he would ever make that film with Ruan Ling-yu.[27]

Notes

1. Li Suyuan and Hu Jubin, *Chinese Silent Film History* (Beijing: China Film Press, 1997), p. 201.
2. Yingjin Zhang, *Chinese National Cinema* (New York, London: Routledge, 2004), p. 31.
3. Paul J. Bailey, *China in the Twentieth Century* (Oxford and New York: Basil Blackwell, 1988), p. 32.
4. Ibid.
5. James E. Sheridan, *China in Disintegration: The Republican Era in Chinese History, 1912–1949* (New York: The Free Press/Macmillian, 1975), p. 181.
6. Paul Clark, *Chinese Cinema: Culture and Politics since 1949* (Cambridge: Cambridge University Press, 1987), pp. 11–2.
7. Cho, *Blooming Flower in Shanghai*, p. 47.
8. Wang Renmei, *Wo de cheng ming yu bu xing: Wang Renmei hui yi lu* (Shanghai: Shanghai wen yi chu ban she: Xin hua shu dian Shanghai fa xing suo fa xing, 1985), p. 151.
9. Ibid., p. 150.
10. Ibid., p. 152.
11. Cho, *Blooming Flower in Shanghai*, p. 47.
12. Li and Hu, op. cit., p. 147.
13. Ibid, p 148.
14. Wang Renmei, op. cit., p. 195.
15. *Encyclopedia of China Film*, Vol. 1, p. 222.
16. Wang Renmei, op. cit., p. 100.
17. Ling He (Shi Linghe), "Sun Yu: His Life and Films," *Zhonghua Tuhua Zazhi* (China Picture Magazine), No. 45, August 1936 in *Griffithiana*, 60/61, October 1997, pp. 155–61.
18. The May Thirtieth Movement denotes the killing of twelve Chinese demonstrators by British troops on May 30, 1925 in Shanghai, followed by the death of fifty Whampoa Military Academy Cadets in an armed engagement with British and French forces in June.
19. *Encyclopedia of Chinese Films*, Vol. 1, p. 204.
20. Wei Haoming, "Playboy Swordsman," *New Silver Star (Xin ying xing)* 16 (1929).
21. Tiang Xing, "The Minxin Studio and Its New Studio (Qian di wei liang hua Minxin)," *Shadow Play Journal* 1.1 (1929).

22. Jubin Hu, "Chinese National Cinema before 1949," (unpublished PhD dissertation, School of Communication, Arts and Critical Enquiry, La Trobe University, Australia, 2001), p. 114.

23. Jay Leyda, *Dianying, Electric Shadows: An Account of Films and the Film Audience in China* (Cambridge, MA: The MIT Press, 1972), p. 365.

24. Li and Hu, op. cit., pp. 217–21.

25. Ibid., pp. 222–3.

26. Richard J. Meyer, *Ruan Ling-yu: The Goddess of Shanghai* (Hong Kong: Hong Kong University Press, 2005), p. 23.

27. Ibid., p. 25.

CHAPTER 3

"The Emperor of Film"

S hanghai in late winter was cold and damp. The hazy sun set early bringing a biting wind chill to those who traveled or slept on the streets. Yet as the 1930s began, the city was at its most prosperous peak.[1] Lianhua studios had investors' money to make films and their stable of directors, actors, and writers possessed some of the finest talent in world cinema.

Sun Yu, although ill, decided to begin filming *Yecao Xianhua* (Wild Flower), which he had written, with Jin Yan and Ruan Lingyu in mind for the leads. The director had been quite demanding when he worked with Ruan on the film *Spring Dream in the Old Capital* which was a box-office success. Sun's method was to ask his actors to really think about the character and of people they had met in their lives who were like them. He knew he was taking a chance with Jin, but one of the director's greatest attributes was to make stars of raw talent.

Both Jin and Ruan appreciated Sun's efforts to come to the studio in terrible weather and continue shooting. The two emerging actors started both a successful professional relationship and a warm close friendship on the set.[2] They were to become the 1930s version of Spencer Tracy and Katharine Hepburn in Shanghai. The pair made seven films together before Ruan's tragic suicide in 1935.

In *Wild Flower*, Jin plays Huang Yun, the son of a wealthy tea merchant and Ruan stars as Li Lian, a poor flower seller. The plot begins with the drought and war in northwest China. It reflected the chaos and tragedy brought about by urbanization and social mobility in the 1920s and 1930s. The opening shots, framed beautifully by Sun, depict a mother holding a baby attempting to cross a frozen river. When the infant cries for food, the starving woman has no breast milk, so she bites her finger and feeds the baby with her blood, and then dies. An old carpenter finds the child and takes her to Shanghai. Sixteen years later, the girl must sell flowers to support her family.

Meanwhile Huang, who has broken relations with his father, the tea merchant, because he did not want to marry a woman his parents had selected, moves into his own apartment. The young man composes music and plays the *qin*. One day while walking, the musician sees Li Lian hit by a passing auto. He takes the girl home and teaches her to sing and play the stringed instrument. Huang writes an opera and gives Li Lian the lead. It is a huge success. The couple becomes engaged and plans to marry. When the tea merchant learns about the impending union, he persuades the girl to end the relationship for the best interests of his son. He tells her that a "wild flower" cannot marry someone from his class. Li Lian leaves Huang and becomes a dancing girl. Not knowing the real facts, the young man lambastes her as a "wild weed and idling flower" and returns home. He later learns the truth and rushes to Li Lian's room at the end of the film.[3]

Wild Flower was extremely important in establishing Jin as a leading man, and he together with Ruan, began a series of box-office hits. The film broke Chinese technical barriers. Sun used crane shots, flexible camera movements, and "many aspects of Europeanization in the metropolitan life of Shanghai." He was censured by some critics for his foreign style, but the public loved the movie. Jin and Ruan sang and played string instruments for "A Long March to Find Brother," written by Sun. It was recorded on a wax disc and played on an amplified phonograph during the film. This was the first time a song from a Chinese movie was ever heard during the screening of a movie.[4]

Lianhua decided to make another film with the pair right away. The studio asked veteran director Bu Wancang and screenwriter Zhu Shilin to come up with another love story. In addition, they used creative cinematographer Huang Shaofen who had shot Ruan in previous movies. The twenty-one-year-old cameraman was the same age as Jin and Ruan. He is credited with developing and using the first soft lens in China, using gauze for the close-up shots.[5]

Bu and Jin became lifelong friends during the making of this new film. The director was older and had more experience than the upcoming star. Here again, Jin found another mentor. Bu had been writing and making movies since 1921 at both the Mingxing and Minxin studios. He had worked with another of the young actor's friends, Tian Han.[6]

Bu's fresh product, *Lian'ai Yu Yiwu* (Love and Duty), was based on a novel of the same name written by Hua Luoshen and based on a Polish story, *La Symphonie des Ombres*. The opening shot has a close-up of a ringing alarm clock with the camera revealing Jin Yan as Li Zhuyi, a lazy student who stays in bed. When the servant finally wakes him, he is late for school. As he rushes to make up for his tardiness, he notices Yang Naifan, played by Ruan Ling-yu. The teenager lives across the street. Each day he follows her. One morning she looks back at him and is struck by an auto. He binds her wounds with his handkerchief. They become close friends. Later, he leaves to attend college overseas.

Yang's father arranges a marriage for his daughter with the wealthy son of an aristocratic family against her wishes. She has two children. Years later, she takes them to a park. One of the youngsters falls into the lake. Li happens to be there and rescues the child. The couple recognize one another and their love is rekindled. After several meetings, Yang decides to run away with Li, leaving her son and daughter. Li is disinherited by his family and has to find work to support his love who bears him a little girl. Working long hours, he contracts tuberculosis and dies. Yang contemplates suicide but decides to raise her daughter by working as a seamstress. In the end she takes her own life and the father of her first two children adopts the child.[7]

Both Jin and Ruan displayed their aging from teenagers to mature adults with remarkable performances. The actors used body language to communicate how they had become old before their years. Jin's death scene as he collapses after a coughing fit was entirely believable. He had learned to be natural and not over-play as some did in silent cinema. His exposure to death and sickness as a child apparently served him well.

When *Love and Duty* was released in early 1931, the public clamored for more of Ruan and Jin. While Lianhua was making plans for additional features starring the new screen couple, Jin was asked to star in a role as a handsome movie star in a film within a film.

The plot is similar to many Hollywood movies of the same period using the device of talent discovered in amateur performances that then go on to stardom in motion pictures or Broadway shows. A plot similar to Hollywood's *A Star is Born* is close to Jin's new production. Nearly the entire Lianhua stable of directors and actors were used in the location shots of a film company on a shoot for *Yin Han Shuang Xing* (Two Stars Shining in the Milky Way). The

"Milky Way" was a Chinese popular term for "silver screen." Jin Yan was now one of the greatest stars in China.

Director Shi Dongshan cast Jin as Yang Yiyun, a handsome and famous star. While filming on location, the entire crew hears a beautiful girl, Li Yueying, played by Zi Luolan, sing a majestic song composed by her father. The director of the film, after listening to the music and the praises of his staff, goes to see her perform. After the curtain falls, he runs backstage and persuades her to become a movie actor.

The Milky Way Film company has Li and Yang star in an opera entitled *Loudong Yuan* (Envy in the Mansion). Yang helps the new actress as she performs in front of the camera. She becomes enamored with her leading man and he thinks about her at his home as he gazes at her photo. Suddenly, he comes across his marriage license of many years ago; his face is convulsed with pain.

Later, Yang decides to avoid Li but she follows him around. When the film is about to be premiered, the company holds a banquet and celebration. The glamorous lifestyles of movie people are portrayed at the dinner, with Yang driving his own convertible to the nightclub. Li and Yang dance a passionate tango with great emotion. The guests are thrilled with their performance.

The plot then enters the realm of moralism. The film's director urges Yang not to waste the youth of Li. The male star feigns sickness to return to his rural home. His old mother is being cared for by the country wife. Faced with the choice of divorcing his old spouse and returning to Li, he chooses duty over love, a common theme in Lianhua melodramas. The actor passes the house where he first heard the young girl sing and listens to her vocalize. He refuses to cause her pain and walks away at the end.[8] It was after this film that people started to compare Jin Yan with Rudolph Valentino because of his dancing and love scenes.

While the filming was almost completed for *Two Stars in the Milky Way*, Bu was preparing Ruan Ling-yu to return in another film with Jin Yan. He asked scriptwriter Huang Yicuo to write a treatment using Shakespeare's *Two Gentlemen of Verona* as a plot, so Huang authored *Yi Jian Mei* (A Spray of Plum Blossoms). This time Ruan and Jin played brother and sister. The male star resplendent in military uniform as Officer Hu Lunting is stationed in Canton. When he is falsely accused of treason, he escapes from confinement and becomes an outlaw, modeled after Robin Hood. His sister flees from Shanghai in a chartered biplane to help save her brother.

Bu used the same cinematographer as he did in *Love and Duty*. The art deco look of the film, together with a modernist design, created a fresh approach for the audience. Jin's swordplay as the outlaw and the Hollywood happy ending made him as well as Ruan into "Western-style" movie stars. Given Jin's background, combat and adventure were perhaps more real than for any other star. In movies, he was now able to win every battle, whereas in life his country was lost perhaps forever.

Lianhua took advantage of his success. Now the rush was on to grind out another follow-up film. Nineteen thirty-one was becoming a stellar year for Lianhua and its founders were proven to be correct in continuing to make silent cinema. Suddenly these films and the one to follow "helped to lay a solid foundation for Lianhua's dominant position in the domestic film circles."[9]

Bu, using the same crew, decided to return to Chinese themes in *Taohua Qi Xue Ji* (The Peach Girl). Jin plays De'en, the handsome son of a wealthy landowner, who falls in love with Lingu, a peasant girl played by Ruan, who resides on his land. The two grow up in different worlds, yet see one another every month when the boy's mother goes to collect the rent.

When De'en invites Lingu to visit him in the city, he tricks her into staying at the home of one of his late father's concubines. He promises marriage after the innocent maiden becomes pregnant. His mother refuses and De'en is forbidden by her to see Lingu again because of class differences. De'en finally comes to Lingu's side as she lies dying. The landowner relents after her death and allows her son to raise the child. The final scene with De'en, his mother, and Lingu's blind father at the tomb shows the reconciliation. The grieving young man looks at the grave and says, "We will meet again on the other side."[10]

The countryside locations were captured by cinematographer Huang as if they were ancient Chinese landscapes. Even the mud fight among the peasant boys was shot in an artistic manner. Bu's contrast between city and country life, peasant and landowner, rich and poor, weak and strong, were illustrated by the superb characterizations of his actors. Ruan, as an innocent milkmaid, displayed naïveté in her every expression and movement, while Jin, as the wealthy scion, moved his body and face to convey weakness, until the scene when he defies his mother and races to his sweetheart's side.

Although Bu communicated that class differences could be overcome by love, this theme was intended to thwart KMT censors. The director and many Lianhua members were part of the left-wing progressive movement which sought to expose the inequities of the society. They used the melodramatic soap opera format to outwit those who would cut scenes from films.

Production of *The Peach Girl* was completed on September 17, 1931. As the cast and crew returned to Shanghai full of enthusiasm for their next project and happy with the results of the shoot, they learned about what happened the very next day in Mukden, Manchuria. The Japanese army had planted a bomb which blew up on the tracks of the Japanese railway. The explosion gave the military an excuse to occupy Manchuria.

Chiang Kai-shek told the Manchurian warlord Zhang Xueliang not to resist the invaders. The generalissimo wanted to save his army to fight the Communists. Soon after, the Japanese placed Puyi, the Manchu, on the throne as emperor of the puppet state of Manchukuo.

The citizens of Shanghai were appalled by the events in the north. They all joined in an anti-Japanese boycott. Japanese goods were not purchased. By the end of 1931 their merchandise dropped to 3 percent of the city's total imported goods from a high of almost one third previously. Most Japanese-operated factories closed or stopped operations on a temporary basis. The Tokyo government was losing its patience with the unruly metropolis.

Jin's co-star suddenly decided to leave the beleaguered city with her lover Zhang Damin and Xiaoyu, her adopted child. Ruan Ling-yu could not witness the instability and anti-Japanese rioting in her beloved Shanghai. Li Minwei, realizing the value of his top actress, provided his home in Hong Kong for her to relieve her anxieties. These pangs of grief were due also to the wayward ways of Zhang, who had stolen money from his employers and was fired. Ruan had to pay off all of his debts.

Jin, anticipating the production of another film with his co-star, asked Sun Yu what his next project without Ruan would be. The director assured him that he had the male lead in his next film and that he had written a major part for his new discovery, Wang Renmei.[11] Sun had discovered the seventeen-year-old singer and actress performing with the Bright Moon Choir. The teenager had studied acting and voice at the Meimei Girls School in Shanghai. Its founder was impresario Li Jinhui, who recognized the girl's talent immediately. After a year at the academy she was asked to tour in a show traveling throughout Southeast Asia organized by Li. In 1929 she returned to study at Meimei and joined the Bright Moon Choir.[12]

Sun, with the casting of Wang as Xiao Feng in *Ye Meigui* (Wild Rose), demonstrated again his prowess in finding and developing inexperienced actors. It is no wonder by 1932 he was to be known as the "poet" of film.[13]

Both Sun and Jin were devastated by the Japanese invasion of Manchuria. They wanted this film to portray the Chinese as strong and to inspire the populace to fight the invaders, yet not be banned by the KMT censors. The new face of Lianhua, Wang Renmei, anxious to please Sun, was thrilled to play opposite a heartthrob like Jin.

Wang as Xiao Feng, or "Little Wind," is the very essence of health, a wild girl full of vigor, who often unbinds her hair and bares her legs. She is headstrong and mischievous. At the beginning of the film, she organizes the children of the district to put on military exercises. The residents call her their wild rose — sweet, beautiful, and fragrant.

Jin as Jiang Bo, a wealthy painter, is driving his expensive convertible to a small fishing village to sketch the countryside. He spots Xiao having an altercation with a rich merchant who is trying to make advances. The girl pushes the lecher into the mud and gets dirt all over her face. The artist stops his car and laughs at the scene. She is not amused. He is captivated by her adorable, fresh, and unsophisticated behavior.

As the story progresses, she agrees to let him paint her portrait. When Little Wind's father has a fight with the merchant and knocks him unconscious, he leaves the hut which later catches fire. The father is accused of murder and disappears. Little Wind is homeless so Jiang brings her back to Shanghai. Before taking her to his home, he stops to buy her city clothes and has her visit a beauty parlor. The scene when she enters the mansion and keeps falling in her new high heels is hilarious. She fascinates the upper-class people in Jiang's home and shocks them with her direct ways of speaking. The guests feel humiliated. Unlike Pygmalion, Jiang cannot convert Xiao from the country lass to a city girl. They are expelled from the house by the artist's father.

The pair, now in love, move into a slum dwelling with two friends. At first they have a happy existence. When winter comes, Jiang becomes ill and they run out of money and face eviction. Little Wind finds the purse of a drunk on the snowy streets and returns home. When the police arrive, Jiang says he took the money and is also accused by the drunk. He is taken to jail. Little Wind goes to Jiang's father and promises to keep away from his son forever if he will help.

When the artist is released she is gone. He returns to his upper-class life after searching for her unsuccessfully. China is being threatened from beyond the oceans. (Japan is never mentioned because of Chiang's policy of appeasement.) At a grand ball held in his mansion, the northeast military volunteer's song is heard from the parade on the street. Hearing the martial music, Jiang yells at the people dancing who had ignored the national crisis. He throws open the window and spies his two old friends from the slums who urge him to join. The young man, attired in a tuxedo, leaps from the room onto the street where he joins the marchers. As he strides with the throng, he notices the back of a female volunteer with long hair. Jiang approaches and discovers it is Xiao Feng. Together they march forward with an army of patriots.[14]

Sun's brilliant direction with magnificent country scenery and shot composition highlighted by beautiful tracking shots communicated the pace of events. The director used overhead shots and a crane to follow Jiang and Xiao up and down the stairs to their flat. In addition to Jin's convertible, he is seen riding a motorcycle. When the film was released in 1932, Wang Renmei was referred to as "Wild Rose." The close working relationship between Jin and Wang soon led to their becoming lovers.

Before audiences could screen *Wild Rose*, the Japanese found another excuse for action. It was perpetrated when Japanese monks were "attacked" by a crowd in the Chinese district of Chapei; one was killed and two wounded. The Japanese consul general presented an ultimatum to the mayor. Arrest those responsible, dissolve all anti-Japanese groups and end the boycott in ten days or else their navy would occupy Shanghai. Chiang Kai-shek acquiesced but Japanese marines invaded anyway in late January 1932. The KMT army fought back, but bombers from Japanese ships destroyed Chapei. After five weeks, a truce was negotiated in May which called for demilitarization.

The conflict, more popularly referred to as the "Shanghai Incident," was a foreshadow to the events five years later when the Japanese invaded Shanghai again and remained for eight years as an occupying force. Although the democracies of the world were outraged in 1932 little was done to come to China's aid. The United States protested but President Hoover informed Japan that he would not resort to economic sanctions.[15]

When Shanghai calmed down at the end of May, Lianhua was ready to re-start its operation. However, due to the crisis, one of its studios was completely destroyed and its output had decreased. In addition, sixteen of the thirty-nine cinema theaters in the city were in ruins. The production company was in deep financial trouble. It needed to produce a moneymaker quickly. They asked Bu Wancang and Zhu Shilin to create a sequel to *Spring Dream in the Old Capital* and insert Jin Yan into the story to be paired with Ruan Ling-yu, who had returned to Shanghai.[16]

Jin agreed, but was more anxious to make an anti-Japanese film written by his old friend and new housemate Tian Han, whose home had been destroyed by the bombing. Wang Renmei had moved in as well. She recalled in her autobiography that she was nervous when she was introduced to Jin's "respectable older brother." Tian brought her, Nie Er, the composer and Jin to observe the actual fighting between the KMT Nineteenth Route Army and the Japanese marines at the North Railway Station. They were impressed as the defenders fought back even after heavy pounding by the invaders' artillery. The battle continued for five weeks until the truce. Jin and Wang wanted to make a patriotic film right away, but he had to complete the production with Ruan.[17]

Xu Gudu Chunmeng (Spring Dream in the Old Capital II) begins where the first film ended. The repentant father, Zhu Jiajie, takes his family from Beijing to their home in Hunan. Ruan, returning to her role as the man's concubine, plays Yanyan, the former prostitute. After her master is forced to work as a coolie by the evil warlord, she is captured trying to escape and is coerced to become the mistress of the commander of the warlord's armies, Qu Huchen. Meanwhile, Zhu's daughter escapes and becomes a nurse in a Red Cross hospital. She meets wounded Huang Guoxiong, played by Jin, who is battalion leader of a group of revolutionary troops. Later Zhu is asked by Qu to assist him since the old man can write. After seeing the evil ways of the warlord, Zhu secretly visits Huang and they plot to overthrow Qu. Yanyan learns of the plan and tells the villain, not knowing that her former master was the perpetrator. Just as Qu is about to shoot Zhu with his crossbow, Huang leads his men and attacks, killing the warlord. The revolutionary soldiers bring peace to Hunan and the family of Zhu Jiajie is reunited again.[18]

With the completion of *Spring Dream II*, Jin could focus on a veiled anti-Japanese film written by Tian. The need for ambiguity was prompted by the KMT's appeasement policy as they did not want to anger the Japanese. The scenario for *San Ge Modeng Nuxing* (Three Modern Women) was inspired by one of the letters Jin had received. He was inundated by thousands of fan missives which were screened by Tian. This long document contained 30,000 Chinese characters with romantic lines imitating eighteenth- and nineteenth-century European novels. The female author from a distant province insisted on coming to Shanghai to see Jin Yan. Tian, using the woman as a model for one of his women, created a melancholic character, Chen Ruoying, who believes love is the most important aspect of life, yet has an empty soul. The scriptwriter wrote a part specifically for Jin as Zhang Yu, which would presage the author's expectations for the young actor.[19] The film was loosely based on the career of the Hollywood of Asia's new screen heartthrob.

Jin had given a copy of the script to Ruan Ling-yu who had never acted in an outright politically tinged film. She was impressed with its nationalistic and anti-Japanese sentiments. Lianhua's leading lady asked director Bu Wancang if she could have one of the leading roles. Jin and Tian were delighted. The author would have liked to direct the film himself, but he was on the KMT police list and Jin had asked his friend Bu to be in charge. Even the author's name had to be changed to Chen Yu to avoid censorship.[20]

Despite the risks, production started on *Three Modern Women*. The plot follows the life of handsome movie star Zhang Yu, played by Jin. He is involved with three "modern" young women, each of whom represents a particular type of lady. The first one, Yu Yu, played by Li Zhuozhuo, is a rich social butterfly who tries to lure him, but fails. The second, Chen Ruoying, played by Chen Yanyan, is a star-struck girl who follows the screen idol until he agrees to make a movie with her. In the film within the film that they appear in together, the script calls for her to commit suicide. During the take, Chen uses a real knife and kills herself. The third woman, Zhou Shuzen, voluntarily played by Ruan, has been engaged to Zhang through an arranged marriage in the northeast. He forgets her after achieving stardom. When the Japanese invade Manchuria, she and her mother flee to Shanghai. Zhou calls Zhang and tells him to help save the country. He realizes that he has been making superficial movies and joins the soldiers defending Chapei as a medic.

Zhang is wounded and in the hospital meets Zhou who is working as a nurse. He falls in love with her again, but the young woman puts him off. The screen star tries to impress her by taking her to dance halls and casinos. It does not work. Then she shows him how factory workers are exploited and the miserable conditions in Shanghai's slums. Zhang becomes aware that his ex-fiancée from an upper middle-class family is now a member of the proletariat. They work together supporting a workers' strike. The new "modern" woman shouts, "We also have two hands, what are we afraid of?" Zhang grabs Zhou's hand and keeps on shaking it for a long, long time as the scene fades to black.[21] The film was a success at the box office. It is considered the first "left-wing movie." *Three Modern Women* became a model for many so-called progressive anti-establishment films which came later.[22]

Reaction to the film was what Jin and Tian had anticipated. Even though critic Hung Shen praised the movie, as did several other writers, as a "new road of courage," the negative response was violent.[23] KMT thugs, known as the "blue shirts," wrecked the entire facility of Tian's other studio Yihua. Leaflets left by the gangsters were sent to all the Shanghai cinemas and published in the press. They stated:

> Films made by Tian Han, Xia Yan, Bu Wancang, Jin Yan [and others named] that promote class struggle, pit poor against rich — such reactionary films [*sic*] may not be shown. If they are shown, there will be violence and we cannot assure you that what happened to the Yihua Company will not happen to you.[24]

Jin was not frightened. He even published a letter to the public "arguing that actors should not be the toys for the bourgeois class, and that actors should serve the society with anti-imperialist enterprise."[25] Wang Renmei also was defiant. She supported her lover and believed that "as long as Jin Yan followed Tian Han he would not be wrong."[26]

Lianhua and the other film companies were threatened to follow the KMT party line, which was appeasement to the Japanese and opposition to the CCP. Jin and his fellow actors were aware of the policy after the treaty with Japan and the KMT's policy of banning "provocative films" that "could finish the peacemaking actions of the government" in 1932.[27]

To ease the tension at the studio and just to get exercise, Jin organized a basketball team. His height as well as his experience in high school made him the natural leader. Luo Mingyou agreed to buy a really expensive basketball and arranged to have a court provided, if they would name the team Lianhua. The actors enjoyed the game and the starting five immediately attracted the attention of the public.[28] According to Wang Renmei, the reason why athletics was so important for actors like Jin Yan was because they regarded sports as a basic training of an actor. Jin also did boxing, rowing, weight-lifting, swimming, shooting, tennis, and soccer. He believed that only those actors enthusiastic about sports would have a sharp mind and quick reflexes. This would help them understand quickly and express accurately the sentiment and mood of the characters they were playing. His team members agreed with him.[29]

While the Chinese Nineteenth Army was retreating from Shanghai after the so-called truce of May 1932, Jin and Bu immersed themselves in a film whose ending reflected their somber moods. *Ren Dao* (Humanity) tells the story of Zhao Minjie, played by Jin, who gives up thoughts of college to stay at home and marry according to his father's wishes. His classmate goes to Tianjin to study and returns to the town, by now an important official, and urges Zhao's father to send him to the university. The old man takes his life's savings and gives it to his son to study. After only six months, the young man is corrupted by "the evil stench of the city" and falls into wretched habits. He chases women and finally becomes involved with Liu Xiyi, the daughter of the manager of an international trading company. He helps her with her homework and she thinks the older student is an excellent scholar. Instead he continues to pursue outside social activities, such as drinking and party-going.

Meanwhile Zhao's father has to sell the family property in order to keep sending funds to support his schooling. The old man does not tell his son because he is worried that the student will be distracted from his academic pursuits. At graduation, Zhao becomes engaged to Liu and her father secures him a position at his company with a big salary. He receives a letter from home asking for help, but instead hesitates as the wedding date approaches. His parents die without him knowing while Zhao's first wife does everything in her power to save the old man unsuccessfully. Things become bleak for the wayward son as his new wife regrets the marriage and begins to have affairs with different men. Zhao cannot take it any more and leaves in a rage. He returns to his ancestral home to discover his parents dead and his first wife dying. He takes her body and buries it next to his father and mother. At the end, the prodigal son stands at the graves with his own boy, disconsolate, not knowing where he will end up.[30]

Jin recalled that this film symbolized for him the disappointment of the Chinese people when the Chinese retreated in 1932. He wrote: "I was there, continuing my own work of numbing myself — this is the last scene of Humanity."[31]

During that summer, when Jin and members of his studio were planning their big anti-Japanese film, Wang went back to the reorganized Bright Moon Society where she continued to be a singing and dancing girl. Jin saw the show and was "unsatisfied." He called Wang and her cohorts "those who flash their thighs in an erotic way for material interest." The actress was furious. She forgave him after she read Jin's article in *Movie Times*. The film star mentioned the Japanese bombing of Shanghai and the Chinese loss. He appealed to the public by writing "that the artillery of imperialists are already aiming at our heads." He argued that "the development of Chinese movies cannot be separated from the actual issues of China, and that the only way out is to unite all social forces to fight with the imperialism that is suppressing us." Wang wrote, years later, that after she saw Jin's piece she "thought that he was a real passionate man" and could not stay angry with him any more. She commented that his behavior in later years never betrayed those ideals expressed in the magazine.[32] She was always his biggest fan.

The public, fueled by anti-Japanese sentiments and adoring of Jin Yan, believed he could do no wrong. He had become the biggest male superstar in Shanghai and audiences, especially women, wanted more. Lianhua asked him to make a quick pot-boiler before the patriotic film. He agreed as long as he could approve the script. Some at the studio considered him arrogant or picky about the material. He was concerned with the content and refused to star in any film that was void of political context. His popularity was enhanced when the newspaper *The Sound of Cinema* launched a poll so readers could elect a "Movie Emperor." Jin Yan was elected in a runaway race.[33] He became known as the "Lianhua Hunk" because of his muscular build and athletic demeanor. Although he was now the highest-paid male movie star in China, the actress Hu Die at competing Mingxing was paid eight times as much.[34]

Women were throwing themselves at Jin at every party and social event. A girl from Hankou fell in love with him watching all of his movies. She journeyed to Shanghai to find him. Bu Wancang and Tian Han intercepted her before she could reach the star. They invited her to dinner and persuaded her to get back on the train and return home.[35] Yet Wang forgave Jin when he cheated on her. She continued to perform with the Bright Moon Society and live with him.[36]

The newly crowned "Emperor of Film" worked with a new director, Jin Qing Yu in the film *Haiwai Juanhun* (Cuckoo's Soul beyond the Seas). Jin plays Zhong Zhigang, a poor clerk in a bookstore, who moves to the Philippines with two friends from Shanghai. The young girl, Yang Qihua, is a music teacher and has known Zhong since childhood and he is in love with her but is the strong and silent type and hesitates to tell her. The other man, Li Daosheng, is the opposite and through a series of slimy activities gets Yang drunk and takes her virginity. Zhong thinks the girl is happy and returns to Shanghai. Yang is pregnant and her secret husband, Li, in the meantime, becomes the son-in-law of a warlord and lives a flamboyant life. Zhong sees this travesty of justice as he learns about Li's perfidy with Yang and denounces him publicly. The villain intends to take revenge on his accuser but loses his footing and falls off a building and dies. Zhong is charged with murder and sentenced to death. Just before the execution he writes a letter to Yang telling her what has transpired. She reads the letter as she dies and her spirit flies out to go hand in hand with that of Zhong.[37] While this melodrama passed the KMT censors without a problem, it clearly showed the injustices of the society and the influence of money over every aspect of life in China at that time.

Jin's political activism continued. Nineteen thirty-two was turning out to be a stellar year for Jin Yan. He and Wang Renmei joined the other left-wing members of Lianhua to make their long-planned anti-Japanese film *Gong Yue Guo Nan* (Going to Aid the Nation Together). The studio was a divided entity. Progressive anti-establishment films were produced side-by-side with pro-KMT ones. The censors were outwitted by the creativity and ideals of the leftists. They disguised the political nature of the plots and presented them as melodramatic soap operas. The messages were clear, but the endings held to the KMT party line.[38] In addition, studio boss Luo Mingyou was very loyal to the KMT government and supported Chiang's New Life Movement which advocated a return to Confucian lifestyles.

Going to Aid the Nation Together was sometimes referred to as "Onward Together to Face the Country's Hardships." The plot is simple. It relives the events of the Japanese invasion of Manchuria and its subsequent bombing of and aggression in Shanghai. Directors Cai Chusheng, Sun Yu, and others present a montage of Japanese soldiers advancing south of the Yangtze River to threaten Shanghai. After they bomb the city, the aggressors are held off by the Nineteenth Route Army. There is a conflict between those who support the KMT position of appeasement and those who want to fight. One line from the film gives its message: "The war is unfortunately upon us. It is the very time that we ought to rise to the aid of our country." At the close, a brother of one who was killed and had hesitated in fighting the Japanese joins the militia to save the country and heads to the front lines. Jin played one of the militia and Wang is seen as a civilian caught up in the chaos. The rest of the cast included most members of the Lianhua troupe.[39] Ruan wanted to participate but was experiencing personal problems. Her colleagues understood and assumed that she could make other progressive films after this one. Sun Yu told her he was writing one especially for her and Jin promised to make his next film with Ruan. Her depression was eased when her lover went away to Fujian because now she could concentrate on her career.[40]

Jin Yan looked forward to 1933 as the newly crowned Emperor. His press reviews were excellent, the public was thrilled with his work, and he had managed to stay out of trouble with the KMT mainly due to his popularity. The approaching new year would come to be known as "Chinese Film Year" and Jin Yan and his costar Ruan Ling-yu were the major reasons. Both of them agreed to appear in a film about the class struggle and squalid conditions in the slums of Shanghai. They were eager to work with newly hired Fei Mu, whose reputation as a film critic and writer preceded him. The fledgling director did not disappoint them. His debut film, *Cheng Zhi Ye* (City Nights) was critically acclaimed. The anti-establishment activities of Jin and Ruan continued mostly unabated.

Notes

1. Stella Dong, *Shanghai: The Rise and Fall of a Decadent City* (New York: HarperCollins, 2000), p. 209.
2. Meyer, *Ruan Ling-yu*, p. 25
3. *Encyclopedia of Chinese Films,* p. 255.
4. Li and Hu, *Chinese Silent Film History*, p. 281.
5. Harriet Sergeant, *Shanghai* (London: Jonathan Cape, 1991), p. 288.
6. Leyda, *Dianying, Electric Shadows*, p. 370.
7. *Encyclopedia of Chinese Film*, p. 32.
8. Ibid., p. 42.
9. Li and Hu, op. cit., p. 225.
10. *Encyclopedia of Chinese Cinema,* p. 38.
11. Wang Renmei, *Wo de cheng ming yu bu xing: Wang Renmei hui yi lu* (Shanghai: Shanghai wen yi chu ban she: Xin hua shu dian Shanghai fa xing suo fa xing, 1985), p. 103.
12. Ibid., p. 267
13. Li and Hu, op. cit., p. 346.
14. Wang Renmei, op. cit, p. 104.
15. Barbara W. Tuchman, *Stillwell and the American Experience in China, 1911–45* (New York: Grove Press, 1970), p. 137.
16. Meyer, op. cit., pp. 33–4.

17. Wang Renmei, op. cit., p. 150.
18. *Encyclopedia of Chinese Film,* p. 70.
19. Wang Renmei, op. cit., p. 152.
20. Leo Ou-fan Lee, "Urban Milieu of Shanghai Cinema," in Zhang (ed), *Cinema and Urban Culture in Shanghai, 1922–1943* (Stanford: Stanford University Press, 1999), p. 85.
21. *Encyclopedia of Chinese Film*, p. 64.
22. Laikwan Pang, *Building a New China in Cinema: The Chinese Left-Wing Movement, 1932–1937* (Lanhan, MD: Rowman and Littlefield, 2002), p. 44.
23. Hung Shen, *Works*, Vol. 4 (Peking, 1963), trans. Jay Leyda, *Dianying, Electric Shadows*, pp. 87–8.
24. Leyda, op. cit., p. 88.
25. Wang Renmei, op. cit., p. 153.
26. Ibid., p. 153.
27. Leyda, op. cit., p. 88.
28. Wang Renmei, op. cit., pp. 165–6.
29. Ibid., p. 173.
30. *Encyclopedia of Chinese Film,* p. 63.
31. Wang Renmei, op. cit., p. 195.
32. Ibid., p. 267.
33. Ibid., p. 195.
34. Jeff Yang, *Once upon a Time in China* (New York: Atria Books, 2003), p. 15.
35. Yingjin Zhang, *The City in Modern Chinese Literature and Film: Configurations of Space, Time, and Gender* (Stanford: Stanford University Press, 1996), p. 315.
36. Cho, *Blooming Flower in Shanghai*, pp. 51–2.
37. *Encyclopedia of Chinese Film,* pp. 56–7.
38. Meyer, op. cit., p. 41.
39. *Encyclopedia of Chinese Films,* pp. 50–1.
40. Meyer, op. cit., p. 36.

CHAPTER 4

The Japanese Strike

The up and coming director Fei Mu, while delighted to have Jin Yan and Ruan Ling-yu assigned to him for his debut film at Lianhua, decided to shock the audience. The director cast Jin in his first role as a screen villain. Fei, who had been educated in a French school in Beijing, was a famous writer before his move to Shanghai in 1932. His directorial bow a few months later with *City Nights* was critically acclaimed. The film concerns class tensions between workers and capitalists with a clear bias for the working poor.

Ruan plays the daughter of a sick coolie who works on the fetid docks of Shanghai. They live in a slum owned by a capitalist who plans to demolish the area to make way for a dog-racing club. The rich man's son, played by Jin, demands the girl's body in exchange for a delay in the redevelopment. When her father learns about the liaison, he weeps as a great flood of rain comes down on their hovel, "drowning out all sounds of laughter or crying, continually drowning out the sorrow in everyone's heart …"[1]

The story is clearly about class struggle. However, another ending was inserted to get by the KMT censors. At the film's superadded conclusion, the rich man's son joins with the coolie's daughter to seek a new life in the country.[2] Jin, satisfied with the main points of the production and its depiction of the poor, agreed to the phony ending.

But there were other threats to their artistic integrity. Lianhua studios, which had pioneered using wax recordings in theaters in 1930 but continued to make silent films, now felt audio competition from Mingxing. By 1933, plans were made to produce synchronized songs by using the lip-synched method. These early sound motion pictures "hardly attended to dialogue, but rather focused on inserting musical numbers into narrative space or simply used them to display the aural spectacle."[3]

Jin Yan had a natural singing voice which had been demonstrated when he made the recording with Ruan Ling-yu for Sun Yu in *Wild Flower*. The song "A Long March to Find Brother" had been reproduced by the Great China Recording Company accompanied by the Carlton Theater Orchestra, using a combination of Chinese and Western instruments. The records sold well, and greatly added to the film's popularity. The disc's appeal was "that everyone could learn to sing like film stars, if not act like them. The theme song could be acquired separately from the film and be played over and over again in one's living room, thus triggering a gradual yet profound transformation in the structure of cinematic experience as a whole."[4]

While Sun was busy directing Ruan in *Little Toys,* Bu Wancang made a partial sound film with Jin in which the actor could play an aging father as well as the same man as a young revolutionary in several flashback scenes. Chen Yanyan was selected as the "Emperor's" co-star. The actress had a beautiful voice and along with Ruan and Hu Die was one of the most famous stars of the era.[5] Chen played Xiao Mei or "Little Plum" while Jin was cast as Jia Hu.

The combination worked. The opening sequence of *Mu Xing Zhi Guang* (Maternal Radiance) has Little Plum singing a new tune composed by her musician father. Her beautiful looks and musical talent enthrall the guests among whom are the manager of a theater and the boss of a record company. The two want to have her perform on the stage and make a record. Xiao's father is thrilled and tells her to sign the contract. The girl's mother is worried, however, as she wanted her daughter to continue with her education. Her father had been missing for years. As the camera focuses on a photograph of a young Jia Hu, the story flashes back to an earlier time when, as a revolutionary, he had to flee from the police and leave his young wife and little girl. His final words were to ask his spouse to educate the youngster.

The movie reveals the dilemma facing Chinese women. The mother must remarry in order to support herself and her daughter. She does not tell Little Plum who her real father is. Years later, Jia returns from the South Seas, where he has been working in the mines. In another flashback, he is seen bare-chested breaking rocks in the quarry. A later scene has him beaten by an overseer. The revolutionary's daughter is now a famous star so Jia Hu attends her big concert and meets his former wife. He understands the reason for her new marriage and insists that Little Plum not be told that he is her real father. In a twist of fate, he is asked to sing by the master of ceremonies. Jia performs a song from the mines about the difficult life of the workers. The audience is moved. Little Plum asks her new "father" to introduce her to him. When the beautiful young woman stands in front of Jia Hu, he is touched deeply and leaves quietly, holding back his tears.

Meanwhile Little Plum's stepfather marries her off to the son of the wealthy owner of the mine where Jia Hu worked years before. The newlyweds leave for the South Seas where her husband immediately falls for a singing girl and casts aside his bride, who is pregnant. After giving birth, she becomes ill and wires her mother to come. The mother arrives and tells her daughter the truth about her real father. Both weep together. Little Plum divorces her playboy husband and returns to Shanghai with her mother. They join Jia at an orphanage which he operates and assist him with his work. Little Plum gives a concert to raise funds for the parentless children. Her baby dies just before the performance and she walks on the stage holding the dead child. "Her sad song, her eyes welling with tears of blood, deeply moves the hearts of all the audience."[6]

This Lianhua melodrama easily passed the censors. It was another success of recasting social commentary in the form of romantic tragedy. Jin's song of the miners carried revolutionary lyrics written by Tian Han with music composed by Nie Er.[7] The "tear jerker" also criticized the exploitation of the workers as well as the unfairness of the mine's owner and his son. Although there is a morbid ending, the orphanage continues its good work helping poor children. Bu and other directors made sure that Jin Yan had a few scenes in which he appeared bare-chested. The muscular actor was an attraction to female moviegoers.

Off-screen, things were changing for Jin Yan as well. Both he and his lover Wang Renmei were preparing to participate in new sound films for Lianhua. Towards the end of 1933, Wang starred in Cai Chusheng's production of *Yu Guang Qu* (Song of the Fishermen) and Jin played the lead in Sun Yu's *Da Lu* (The Big Road). The audio system was improved thanks to three American-trained radio engineers who had constructed their own sound camera and had founded the Dien Tung Equipment Company, Ltd., to sell and rent film gear. Their technical help increased the success of the studio's new sound films.[8]

As shooting neared completion on both productions, Jin and Wang decided to marry. Jin wanted a simple and modest affair, "not like those of other stars." On the day of the wedding, Lianhua held a 1934 New Year's party. The couple came to the occasion wearing ordinary blue coats. When the bell for the coming year rang, they pulled red velvet cards from their pockets as Sun Yu announced that they were husband and wife. Wang recalled that their simple, modest wedding became a legend among young students of the time. Unfortunately, Lianhua's chief did not agree. He believed that once a female movie star married, she would lose her audience. Wang's contract with the studio was not renewed, but she was able to finish the filming of *Song of the Fisherman*.⁹ She also did not seek employment with other film companies because she was pregnant. Although she decided to rest at home instead of working, the active woman continued to play basketball and swim.

Jin was shooting *The Big Road* on the night Wang had her baby. He rushed to her side the next morning and stayed with her all day. He was happy about the birth of the child and disappointed and sad when the infant died ten days later. Wang blamed a premature delivery for the demise of their son.¹⁰

But the battle with the censors continued. Director Sun Yu was determined to make an anti-Japanese film and still get it by the KMT censors. He often came to Jin's house to discuss the plot of the script for *The Big Road*. The director asked left-wing composer Nie Er to write a song for the film with a tune and a rhythm similar to the Volga Boatman's song. Nie sang it for Jin in the star's living room since he would be vocalizing it in the film. Jin suggested that he raise the pitch of two words to make the song more intense. The idea was taken by the composer.¹¹

Nie Er's music and especially his songs spoke for different oppressed groups. One of the innovations of the composer and his lyric-writing collaborators such as Tian Han and Sun Yu was that they almost invariably chose to write of the struggle of workers, oppressed women and exploited children in terms of a collective "we." *The Big Road*'s song performed by Jin and his fellow road builders is typical of this genre.[12] Nie also wrote a song for Ruan Ling-yu's film *New Woman* that same year. His last composition, "March of the Volunteers" sung by Wang Renmei in the film *Daughter of Wind and Cloud,* was first adopted by the Eighth Route Army and later became the official anthem of the People's Republic of China. In 1935, he escaped to Japan, avoiding arrest by the KMT police. On a beach excursion in July of that year, the young composer drowned.[13]

Jin Yan plays Brother Gold in *The Big Road*. He is one of six men who are roaming workers building roads. They are dedicated to working together to improve the country. They sing Nie Er's song as they use ropes, pass over dangerous mountain passes, ford treacherous streams, and are torn by sharp prickles. They unite their efforts to roll the earth flat and to expand the existing road. In this socialist realism setting influenced by Soviet films, they are pioneers of a new road, brave path-breakers, heroes for all time, spirits filled with fire, forging ahead in unity. Sun Yu's lyrics bring out these themes.

During a daring scene for a 1934 Chinese film, Jin and his pals take a break from their arduous work when they see a pristine river and throw off their clothes and plunge into the water. There is much playfulness and splashing among the men until they spot two young girls sitting on a cliff overlooking the scene. The females, played by Chen Yanyan and Li Lili, who work at the canteen where the road builders eat, shout down that they have watermelons for sale. Sun handled the sequence with humor and cute touches. As the males emerge from the river to climb the hill, the film cuts back to the young women, and then back to the road builders scampering to the top, but with their trousers on. Jin, as usual, has no shirt.

In the film, Brother Gold is the strong leader imploring his men to increase their efforts and quickly repair a strategic military road which will enable the Chinese army to fight the Japanese invaders. Spies from the enemy destroy the work on the roads. Traitorous Chinese try to threaten and bribe the workers. Brother Gold and his six comrades are captured by agents of the enemy and tortured. They are saved by Chen and Li when they smuggle a pair of scissors into the hole where the men are being held. Brother Gold uses his feet to cut the rope binding him and frees the others after a fight with the guards. One of the six is killed in the melee. A crowd of other road workers and townspeople seize the traitors as they attempt to escape. Brother Gold hands them over to the army for trial and the men go back to completing the road.

The final sequence depicts enemy planes bombing the road and strafing the workers. Brother Gold and his fellow workers are killed, but not before the hero shoots down a Japanese plane with a rifle. In a surrealistic climax, spirits of the dead road builders emerge from their limp corpses and sing "Song of the Big Road" as convoys of Chinese trucks brimming with troops use the road to advance on the enemy.[14]

The film was released on New Year's Day 1935 to great acclaim as an anti-Japanese movie in Shanghai and later in other parts of China. The bathing scene where the girls watched the men furtively became a conversation piece all over the country. *The Big Road* is considered one of the top hundred Chinese films of all time. Jin's performance and Sun's direction gave both added stature to their reputations.[15]

Commercial success gave the young couple new confidence. After Wang and Jin recovered from the loss of their child and before the release of *The Big Road* and *Song of the Fisherman,* they decided to appear together in a play written by their friend Tian Han. *The Song for Returning Spring* had music composed by Nie Er. The story was about the Japanese bombing of Shanghai in 1932. Wang played the part of an overseas Chinese girl, Mei Niang, and Jin starred as Gao Weihan, a patriotic young teacher who was injured in the January 28 event, and lost his memory. He regains his sanity later in the drama. Wang sang several songs written in the style of Southeast Asia. She had visited that area earlier in her career as a member of the Bright Moon Choir and did not feel they were difficult for her to vocalize. Jin, hearing her rehearse, was not satisfied with Wang's rendition. He played his guitar and sang her songs repeatedly, telling her how to interpret the details. Jin made his wife practice a long time before he was satisfied. He, too, sang in the play and Wang remembered what a great voice her husband had.[16]

While performing in *The Song for Returning Spring*, Jin decided to appear in a film produced by the Yihua studios which had recovered from the attack by KMT thugs the previous year. Tian had written a script with his actor friend in mind called *Huang Jin Shi Dai* (Golden Age). Bu Wancang directed this left-wing story criticizing the educational system. The author "revealed that education was another form of class struggle." The film was labeled as "Red" by two organizations at the time: the Communist Eradication Association for Chinese Cinema set up at the end of 1933 and the Communist Eradication Association for Chinese Youth, in the beginning of 1934. Director Bu was listed as a "reactionary." The production was affected by these charges. When the film was released, it had gone through several revisions and cuttings by censors. Jin remarked, "The body still exists, but the soul is gone." Yihua suffered a huge loss as the box-office turnout was a failure.[17] By 1935, the studio was forced to produce so-called "soft-films" to stay in business. This resulted in an exodus of the left-wing intellectuals who published an open letter to Yihua in several newspapers criticizing its production policies "and claimed that the recent commercialization of the company completely betrayed its earlier commitment and accomplishments in the new Chinese cinema."[18]

Golden Age has a convoluted plot about how wealthy college students live a fast life which is a trend of modern society. They believe that "youth never comes again" and "life must be lived to the fullest" to develop a philosophy of life based on pleasure. Jin Yan plays a student, Chang Chun, who at first is a playboy but under the influence of a dedicated professor changes his ways. The school for poor people which the old man started stops running. On his death bed, the aged teacher exhorts Chang to continue his posthumous work. The reformed man starts a school with a classmate, Zhang Xiaomei, for the common people. In a fight with a local bandit, Chang is fatally injured. As he draws his last breath, he enjoins his friends to work hard to propagate civilization. When the school opens, Zhang stands in front of the students and tells them "to use their 'Golden Age' to study hard and absorb the rich contents of education for the sake of themselves and the glory of their race."[19] Tian also wrote the lyrics for the theme song of the film, "Yangtze River's Rainstorm."[20]

The KMT was now cracking down on artistic opposition more than ever. During the run of the play in the fall and early winter of 1934, Tian Han sneaked into several performances under cover as he was hiding from the KMT police who were trying to arrest him. He told Jin how satisfied he was with both of their acting and singing presentations. Unluckily, Tian was captured the day after

New Year's in 1935 and sent to Nanjing. Jin did not learn about his friend's imprisonment until a few months later. A woman had broken into the couple's living room, knelt down before Jin, and started kowtowing, saying, "Please find a way to save Tian Han!" Wang recalled: "We were all surprised. I saw Jin Yan's face turn pale; he asked what was wrong, and the woman stood up and we saw that she was Tian Han's lover."[21]

The couple tried to get Tian out of jail from Shanghai, but failed. However, the Lianhua team which had changed its name to the No-name Basketball team was invited to go to Nanjing for a game. Jin was delighted to go along with the group. He told Wang that he intended to find a way to save Tian, seizing this opportunity to travel to the capital city. The screen hero became a real life man of courage and went to see Wang Jinsheng, a junior official of the Public Relations Department of the KMT. Jin never related to anyone the details of his meeting with the KMT officer, but Tian was released shortly afterwards and lived in Nanjing near the home of Wang Jinsheng. It was said that the PR official was an acquaintance of many theater people and he was seen accompanying Tian on trips outside of Nanjing.[22]

During one of the basketball games in Nanjing, while Jin was attempting to rescue Tian, the spectators asked the team to perform after the contest. The actor/players formed a circle and sang "The Song of the Big Road." The audience applauded loudly. They spotted Wang Renmei in her seat and called for her to sing "The Song of the Fisherman," which she did. Both teams were thrilled with the performance.[23]

Other pressures added to their already harried life. While the newly married couple was in Nanjing, they learned about the suicide of their acting colleague, Ruan Ling-yu. Before midnight on March 7, one of the greatest actresses in Chinese history took an overdose of sleeping pills and died the next day. Wang and Jin were shocked. They knew that Ruan had been depressed but could not believe that she had taken her own life at the peak of her career. The pair rushed back to Shanghai for her funeral which was the largest in that city's history. Between 100,000 and 300,000 people lined the ten-mile route from the funeral home to the cemetery where she was buried. Fellow progressives blamed the feudalistic nature of the society for her demise.[24]

Screen legend Hu Die, known as "Butterfly Wu," received a telegram from Shanghai in her Moscow hotel room, informing her of Ruan's death. She was heavy-hearted and when accepting China's first international film award for *Song of the Fisherman* at the 1935 Moscow International Film Festival, spoke a few words about Ruan and her work. Hu was accompanied by the Chinese Classical Theater Troupe and its star Mei Lan-fang. Sergei Eisenstein, the great Soviet filmmaker, was in attendance at the ceremony and later went to a performance of Mei's company. The director filmed one of the episodes and later told the actor that there were similar aspects of realism used in the Russian theater that can be found in the Chinese theater. Eisenstein wondered why Chinese cinema could not be inspired by these qualities.[25]

Wang Renmei was delighted that the film in which she had sung and starred in won this prestigious award. Jin was upset that the KMT had banned showing of *The Big Road*. He also learned that Lianhua was planning to make pro-Nationalist government films and was having financial problems. Its founder, Luo Mingyou, was loyal to the KMT and persuaded Ruan Ling-yu to make a film supporting the New Life Movement just before she died. The studio also failed to raise enough capital because of the worldwide depression.[26]

Jin was ready for a new challenge. Flamboyant impresario and producer Zhang Shankun recruited Jin and director Bu Wancang and others from Lianhua for his newly formed film company Xinhua (New China Movie Enterprises) Productions. The showman received funding from the gangster-operated Great World Amusement Hall and the Gongwutai Opera House.[27] He had the reputation of a rogue businessman who also was a member of the notorious Shanghai mafia organization known as the "Green Gang." Zhang sometimes invested in good movies, but he also did not hesitate to produce "quick and dirty" pictures with, as one critic recalled, "unhealthy content."[28]

Most of all, the boss of Xinhua was best known for his production of *Yeban Gesheng* (Song at Midnight), China's most famous horror film. When the movie opened in Shanghai in 1935, it received the largest publicity campaign in the city's history. A huge coffin was placed outside of the theater with green bulbs in the eyes of a ghostlike face that lit up when people passed by. The tabloid press reported that a child "died of fright" after seeing the film. The plot was adapted from *Phantom of the Opera*. Its protagonist, Song Danping, was a hero in the Republican revolution. His face is disfigured in a fire set by an enemy. At the end of the film, he seeks revenge and kills the foe. Song is burnt by a fearful mob who is scared of his hideous face. As he is enveloped in flames, the weird figure jumps into the sea. Critic Laikwan Pang wrote that almost all of the revolutionary messages delivered by Song were conveyed on the stage in order to present the material as politically correct.[29]

Jin was more ardent that anyone. He was eager to work with a well-known liberal playwright Ouyang Yuqian who had devised a way to elude the censors as he directed *Xin Tao Hua Shan* (New Peach Blossom Fan). He substituted corrupt warlords of the 1920s for the KMT government of the 1930s.[30] Ouyang created the character of Fong Yuming for Jin. The young man is the editor of the newspaper *The People's Way* which advocates the overthrow of the power of the warlords. The evil military governor wants to eliminate Fang by involving him with a famous theater star, Xie Sufang. However, the plan fails as Xie falls in love with the journalist and becomes a revolutionary propagandist in the theater. The governor arrests Xie and sends her to a nunnery where she feigns insanity. The actress is wounded in an insane asylum where she has been sent. At a hospital, she recovers and discovers Fang who had been wounded at the front. They renew their revolutionary fervor as Fang decides to go back and fight despite his wounds. Before his departure, they sing a love song that Xie had written. They dream, after the victory of the revolution, of performing the song together in an opera called *The New Peach Blossom Fan*.[31]

Although this violently anti-KMT film was full of clichés, the audience loved it. Xinhua's so-called "national defense cinema" struck a cord in the movie-going public. Wang Renmei was offered a contract with the studio in 1936 and made one film before she joined her husband to star in *Zhuang Zhi Ling Yun* (Soaring Aspirations). The man chosen to direct this was Wu Yonggang, who had made his debut with Ruan Ling-yu's most famous film *The Goddess*. He advocated unity among the Chinese and armed resistance against foreign invaders. The Hollywood-trained director who had used symbolism to portray the misery and hopelessness of China in Ruan's film now was determined to exploit the talents of Jin and Wang to represent the willingness of the common people to fight Japanese aggression.

In *Soaring Aspirations*, Wang plays Black Girl and Jin her lover, Shun Er. The pair has migrated with a multitude of poor farmers from the drought-ridden plains near the Yellow River to the affluent city of Beijing. They are forced to leave the metropolis and travel to a strange and forlorn area. There, the group of refugees work together for ten years to build a beautiful home called "Peace Village." Wu, using a variety of cinematic devices such as long tracking shots, romantic views of the ripe fields of Sorghum and wipes to change scenes, demonstrated his background as an art designer. He has Wang sing a pastoral song during harvest.

Bandits begin to attack the village. This time the villagers have had enough. They remember the days when roving bands of the warlords drove them out of their homes. They choose Shun to be their leader. With his infectious smile and fierce resolve, he rallies the peasants to resist. In a symbolic scene, the flag of the Republic of China (KMT) is raised over the village. The villagers defiantly defend their home and keep the flag flying despite a dense artillery barrage. The enemy surrounds Peace Village, but in a bloody battle, they are forced to withdraw. Black Girl and many inhabitants are killed. The village is in ruins. The remaining villagers vow to fight on to the end to protect their land. Cannon fire erupts again. Shun shows the farmers how to use rifles to fight the invaders. One can see that Jin is comfortable handling weapons. At the climax, the men grab their guns and call for the enemy to attack. Shun shouts, "If we retreat, where would we go? This is our land."[32]

Wu deliberately used the KMT flag to goad the Nationalist government to stand up to the Japanese instead of fighting the Communists who by this time had reached Yan'an after the Long March. Mao Zedong, their leader, had convinced the European community and many Chinese that "the defeat of Japan took precedence over social revolution because it was necessary first to defeat foreign imperialism and win independence; only then could the struggle for socialism succeed." He told American journalist Edgar Snow that the CCP would be willing to join forces with the KMT against the Japanese.[33]

The films reflected the sentiments of China's intellectuals. Student protests in Shanghai, Beijing, and other cities called for resistance to the invaders of Manchuria. More anti-Japanese boycotts were being organized. Jin and his fellow actors supported the students and endorsed the National Salvation Association founded by Lu Xun and Madame Sun Yat-sen. The group coordinated the nation-wide resistance to Japan. Chiang Kei-shek ignored the outcry.[34]

During this new turmoil, the No-name team continued to participate in the life of Shanghai. The 1936 final game of the Basketball Tournament of Western Shanghai was won by Jin's team. Before the contest, the whole group went to their home and Wang made noodles for them. After the game, Jin Yan received the "silver shield" on behalf of No-name to wild applause by the crowd.[35] Everyone believed it was good for the morale of the metropolis to continue with sporting activities.

Finances at Lianhua were beginning to improve as Luo Mingyu found more investors. A fresh company was formed to manage the production and distribution of its films. This new structure did not affect the quality of its output. Former directors and actors returned to the company including Jin Yan, Sun Yu, Fei Mu, and Wu Yonggang.[36] Jin was pleased to be working again with Sun Yu and actress Li Lili in *Dao Ziran Qu* (Back to Nature).

Sun based the film on J. M. Barrie's play, *The Admirable Crichton*, about an English butler who helps an upper-class family survive after being shipwrecked on a desert island. The director's drama classes in the United States provided him with the tools to adapt this commentary about social class structure from Victorian Britain to Republican China.

Jin Yan stars as Ma Long, a servant to General Zhou played by Lianhua's favorite villain, Zhang Zhizhi. Zhang's daughter, Li Hua, is delightfully interpreted by Li Lili. The plot begins with the general espousing "freedom and equality" for all to modernize China, yet taking advantage of the servant girls of his household and spoiling his three daughters with a decadent lifestyle. Ma accompanies the daughters and their friends on a boating trip. The yacht founders on the rocks and the group is stranded on a desolate island. Suddenly, they must depend on the servant who had been overlooked by the rich travelers. The former servant becomes the leader and forces the upper class survivors to grow crops, weave clothing, hunt for food, and work industriously. The former selfish and arrogant Li Hua is transformed. She can now climb cliffs, swim in deep water, and capture wild animals for food. Ma changes his view of Li, and they fall in love.

The inhabitants of the island are happy with the couple's announcement of their engagement, that is, until a naval ship appears on the horizon. When the band is rescued, they revert to their former arrogant selves. Back in civilization, they once again treat Ma as a servant and expect him to serve them. He is no longer willing to work for the general in that capacity and joins up with the revolutionary armies in the south. In a Hollywood ending, Li Hua bravely goes with him to join up.[37]

During the filming of *Back to Nature,* the No-name team represented Western Shanghai in the all-city finals. The basketball team played Hualian, one of the best five in the metropolis. In the last few seconds of the game, before a capacity crowd, No-name was behind by one point. Fellow Lianhua actor Liu Qiong passed the ball to Jin, who stood alone under the net. The fans went crazy. To everyone's surprise, Jin did not shoot, but passed the ball as the buzzer sounded. No-name lost the game by one point. The team members surrounded Jin and complained. The star explained that in permitting Hualian to win, he was ensuring that the best all-Chinese team could beat the upcoming opponents composed of gangsters and foreigners. He knew that Hualian had a better squad that would secure victory for his countrymen. Jin's leadership skills persuaded his mates to agree with his judgment.[38]

Jin no doubt believed that a healthy body was part of political resistance. The actor's athletic body was healthy and strong. When he was shooting the next film for Lianhua, director Wu Yonggang asked Jin to jump into the river to evade a detective. The weather was freezing in Shanghai, but Jin survived the plunge although he was shivering after the take. A police dog that followed him into the water did not fare as well. The pregnant canine shivered and aborted its fetus.[39]

In his quest to push the barriers of resistance films, Wu decided to make what today one would call an existentialist film. The director opens with shots of waves washing the sand using each wave to eradicate the titles. He begins *Lang Tao Sha* (Two Skeletons/Waves Washing the Sand) with an iris shot exposing two skeletons handcuffed together. In a series of flashbacks, Jin as a merchant seaman discovers his wife in bed with another man. He loses control and kills the adulterer. From then on he has to flee, always pursued by a police detective played by Zhang Zhizhi.

Both men are shipwrecked on a desert island. The sailor rescues the detective from the sea and even though he has a pistol decides not to kill him. He tells the cop his story and the law enforcement officer is moved. When they see a ship, the detective knocks out the mariner and clasps handcuffs on him. The ship sails away and both men await their fate as the waves wash ceaselessly over the sand.[40] The film was attacked by left-wing critics as reactionary and as a mouthpiece for the KMT to present a harmonious and caring society.[41] *Two Skeletons* "suggests that the relationship between human beings is determined by given circumstances." The detractors said the movie denied the existence of class struggle.[42]

Political changes, however, would soon make the lives of Jin and his colleagues even more perilous. In December 1936, Chiang Kai-shek, tired of the CCP's propaganda campaign, flew to Xian to rebuke Chang Hsueh-liang for failing to fight the Communists. The young commander of crack Chinese Manchurian troops instead wanted to engage the occupiers of his homeland in battle. In a move that shocked the world, Chiang was kidnapped and imprisoned by Chang, which became known as The Xian Incident. The generalissimo was presented with a demand that he join forces with the CCP in a united front against the Japanese. Some of the captors wanted the KMT leader shot. In an irony of history, Zhou Enlai, whose friends and family had been massacred by Chiang, suggested that only a coalition or united front, led by his former enemy, could unify the country against Japanese aggression. Realizing that he had no choice, the KMT boss agreed to the Manchurian warlord and the Communists' terms. He was released on Christmas Day.[43]

The United States and European countries were impressed with this new wave of national unity. The Japanese however, read into the move as an obstruction to their "peaceful advance" into China. Militarists in Tokyo began to press for direct action.[44] Six months later on July 7, 1937, Japanese troops skirmished with Chinese soldiers at the 800-year-old Marco Polo Bridge just outside Beijing. The invaders used the so-called kidnapping of one of their privates as an excuse. Although the serviceman was later found in a brothel and returned by the Chinese to his commander, it was too late. Thousands of Japanese troops poured into northern China. The Marco Polo Bridge Incident gave the invaders an excuse to begin the "undeclared war" against China.[45] The full-scale Japanese attack had begun.

Notes

1. *Encyclopedia of Chinese Films,* p. 76.
2. Meyer, op. cit., pp. 36–7.
3. Zhang Zhen, *An Amorous History of the Silver Screen: Shanghai Cinema, 1896–1937* (Chicago and London: University of Chicago Press, 2005), pp. 303–4.
4. Ibid., pp. 314–5.
5. Cho, "The Emperor of Shanghai Movies of the 1930s," p. 210.
6. *Encyclopedia of Chinese Films,* p. 92.
7. Wang Renmei, *Wo de cheng ming yu bu xing,* p. 156.
8. Leyda, *Dianying, Electric Shadows,* p. 95.
9. Wang Renmei, op. cit., p. 154.
10. Ibid., p. 155.
11. Ibid.
12. Andrew F. Jones, *Yellow Music* (Durham and London: Duke University Press, 2001), p. 123.
13. Leyda, op. cit., p. 368.
14. *Encyclopedia of Chinese Films,* p. 144.
15. Cho, *Blooming Flower in Shanghai,* pp. 105–6.
16. Wang, op. cit., p. 156.
17. Li and Hu, *Chinese Silent Film History,* p. 339.
18. Pang, *Building a New China in Cinema,* p. 53.
19. *Encyclopedia of Chinese Films,* p. 117.
20. Cho, *Blooming Flower in Shanghai,* p. 108.
21. Ibid., p. 157.
22. Ibid., p. 158.
23. Ibid., p. 172.
24. Meyer, *Ruan Ling-yu,* pp. 59–64.
25. Leyda, op. cit., pp. 97–8.
26. Li and Hu, op. cit., p. 393.
27. Fu Poshek, *Between Shanghai and Hong Kong: The Politics of Chinese Cinema* (Stanford: Stanford University Press, 2003), pp. 4–6.
28. Wang, op. cit., pp. 193–5.
29. Pang, op. cit., pp. 221–2.
30. Ibid., p. 55.
31. *Encyclopedia of Chinese Films,* p. 166.
32. Ibid., pp. 189–90.

33. Tuchman, *Stillwell and the American Experience in China*, p. 159.
34. Dong, *Shanghai*, p. 249.
35. Wang, op. cit., p. 170.
36. Pang, op. cit., p. 62.
37. *Encyclopedia of Chinese Films*, p. 170.
38. Wang, op. cit., p. 171.
39. Ibid., p. 174.
40. *Encyclopedia of Chinese Films,* pp. 177–8.
41. Pang, op. cit., p. 75.
42. Hu, "Chinese National Cinema before 1949," p. 107.
43. Dong, op. cit., pp. 249–50.
44. Tuchman, op. cit., p. 161.
45. Dong, op. cit., p. 251.

CHAPTER 5

The War Years

One month after the Marco Polo Bridge Incident, Jin Yan and his wife Wang Renmei and the cream of Shanghai's actors appeared in a stage production called "Defending the Lu Gou Bridge." The play was a sensation in Shanghai and was part of a concerted effort by the inhabitants of the city to demonstrate their hatred of the Japanese invasion.[1]

Chinese troops were forming around Shanghai's outskirts as Chiang Kai-shek realized that he could not defeat the Japanese in the north. He hoped that by concentrating his efforts in Shanghai with its large International Settlement, he could induce the Western powers to come to China's aid. By August 12, the invaders sent twenty-six warships up the Huangpu with its flagship, the cruiser *Idzumo*, moored directly in front of the Settlement in clear view of the five-star Cathay Hotel and major shopping thoroughfare Nanjing Road. In addition, thousands of Japanese marines had landed and ousted the Settlement police, declaring authority over all of Hongkou, which was part of the international district. They also evacuated their civilians to Japan.[2]

The Japanese elsewhere continued to target population centers and institutions of higher education in particular. They "systematically and unhurriedly" rained incendiary bombs on Nankai University in Tianjin, because as the press was informed, the school harbored "anti-Japanese elements." The students were considered the most potent agitators of nationalist sentiment. Throughout their campaign in China, as they had done in Korea, "the Japanese intentionally attacked places of education as the source of national consciousness."[3]

Hundreds of thousands started to flee Shanghai. Many Chinese attempted to reach the International Settlement, thinking that the Japanese would not bomb the Westerners' territory. British and American citizens were preparing to board evacuation ships which were being dispatched. Other refugees tried to leave on steamers headed upstream. During this mayhem, Chinese airplanes tried to sink the *Idzumo*, not only missing the target, but dropping bombs on crowded sections of the city, killing and wounding thousands of Chinese and foreigners alike.

Bitter fighting ensued for over two months with the Chinese troops struggling bravely against great odds. Reinforcements from Tokyo gave the invaders a total force of over 200,000 troops. As the battle raged for Shanghai, millions of refugees were forced to sleep on the sidewalks and the lucky ones made it to the International Settlement which was not involved in the battle. Between 1937 and 1939, about 750,000 mainland Chinese fled to this "haven of tranquility." Even after the capture of Shanghai, the Japanese did not take over the Settlements.[4]

By the beginning of 1937, the Japanese had advanced on the capital city of China. They entered Nanjing on December 12 to discover that Chiang and the KMT had departed for Hankou leaving the city undefended. During the next six weeks, Japanese soldiers raped and murdered about 300,000 civilians, with abominable relentless violence.[5] The "Rape of Nanjing" was to become a sore point in the relationship between China and Japan for generations.

Shanghai was spared the same fate because the Japanese only controlled the Chinese portion of the city. The International Settlement including the French Concession remained in European and American hands. These foreign enclaves were surrounded on all sides by the Japanese and were named the "lonely island" and "orphan island." By the end of 1937, it was business as usual in the encircled area whose neutrality was respected by the invaders. Japanese soldiers guarded the entrances to the Settlement and required all Chinese who entered to bow down to them or else they were beaten and even killed.[6]

All of Shanghai's film studios were shut down during the conflagration. As soon as calm was restored, Zhang Shankun reopened his Xinhua facilities and proceeded to hire actors, directors, and crew from the destroyed Mingxing studio and the failing Lianhua Company. While some stars, like Hu Die, fled to Hong Kong, others went to Yan'an or Chongqing. The chief of Xinhua planned "to relaunch the Hollywood of the East."[7] Within two years, the "haven of tranquility," as the Settlement was called, gave employment to 2000 people working in the film industry's almost forty production companies.[8]

Jin and Wang were apprehensive about remaining in Shanghai. Given Jin's political activism in the past, he no doubt felt that they could contribute to their countrymen by continuing to make movies. In addition, Jin had a contract with Xinhua to make several more films. The first one completed, *Wu Song Yü Pan Jin Lian* (Wu Song and Pan Jin Lian), directed by Wu Tsai, was a pot-boiler. Jin is Wu Song, the younger brother of Wu Dalang, who comes to live with Dalang after years away. The elder brother is married to Pan Jin Lian, who immediately falls in love with the good-looking of the two men. She discloses her heart to Wu Song who rebukes her and departs. Pan then has an affair with an official. When her husband discovers the deed, he rushes to take revenge on the adulterer who kicks him down a flight of stairs. The official persuades Pan to poison the injured Wu Dalang and then have his body cremated.

When Wu Song returns, he sees his brother's ashes. Pan again expresses her love for the young man. He refuses her advances once more and discovers the cause of his sibling's death. Full of rage, Wu Song seeks out the official and cuts off his head. He gathers the neighbors together, including Pan, and shows them the bloody skull. In their midst, he excoriates the girl Pan and kills her, thus avenging his brother.[9]

This gruesome remake of an old classic may have been reflecting the massacres taking place all over China. The revenge motif must have been an echo of the Chinese people seeking retaliation against their Japanese oppressors. Even the acting was visceral. Jin got a part for one of his basketball team members, Liu Qiong. The young man had been a law student whose family was bankrupt. Jin encouraged him to become an actor and even coached him. In a scene where Liu was supposed to gasp for air, the novice found it difficult to portray the action. Jin told him to do quite a few pushups. When Liu became exhausted and started gasping, the veteran actor had him run over to the sound stage and play the part. After that the fledging performer became a good actor.[10]

Despite the carnage surrounding them, Zhang Shankun, the wily operator, as usual, developed an advertising campaign for *Wu Song and Pan Jin Lian*. On billboards plastered around Shanghai, he promoted actress Gu Lanjun over Jin Yan. One evening as Jin returned from a dinner with his friends slightly drunk and spied the promotional poster, he pulled down the ad, ripped it up, and smashed the board. Wang Renmei defended his actions by telling people Zhang created the campaign to impress Gu by putting Jin second on the bill. Some people thought the "Emperor" just wanted more fame, but Wang knew his behavior was caused by "an explosion of all the pains and hardship Jin Yan had suffered as an actor longing for social progress."[11]

Business was booming. Shanghai, in 1938, absorbed thousands of new refugees from Europe, mainly Jewish exiles from Germany and Austria, as well as evacuees from other parts of China. The economy of the semi-occupied metropolis thrived as it continued to trade with Southeast Asia, Europe, and the United States. People, film stars, and films themselves moved freely. Approximately 200 movies were produced between 1937 and 1941 and several new cinema theaters were constructed.[12]

Filmmakers, while enjoying profits, had to be even more careful than in the past. There was strict censorship, not only by the Japanese, but by the foreign concession authorities as well. No anti-Japanese or anti-Nazi messages were to be tolerated. In addition, political and violent films were banned. The trend was to produce more entertainment, costume dramas, and historical films in order to pass the censors. Yet, stories about past victories by China against invaders, such as *Hua Mulan Joins the Army* appeared to slip by some officials.[13]

Searching for acceptable plots, Bu Wancang resurrected the 1931 classic *Love and Duty*, which starred Jin Yan and Ruan Ling-yu. The remake *Qing Tian Xue Lei* (Heaven Weeps Tears of Blood) has Jin in his original role of Li Zuyi, and Yuan Meiyun as Yang Naifan, Ruan's part. The director had improved his technical skills in the seven years since the first production. He opens with a montage depicting the beginning of the Republican era in China. Instead of Yang being struck by an auto, the school girl is bitten by a dog on her way to school. Li used his shirt to cover her wound; she keeps the material and he saves the torn shirt for years.

The director made other changes as well. The earlier dream sequence with the duel between Li and her husband was omitted. The young man merely reads about it in a book. Bu uses European abstract shots such as a montage of mouths on the screen to depict gossiping. To change scenes, he employs wipes instead of dissolves. Jin's coughing now can be heard; the actor is convincing as he collapses with tuberculosis. The actress playing Yang is not as beautiful or powerful as Ruan, but Yuan's make-up as the aging seamstress duplicates her performance. In this sound version, the song "Give us back our Mother" is more effective when heard compared with words printed on the title cards. The ending is the same when Yang's ex-husband adopts her daughter to live with his two children.[14]

Even in wartime, Jin's popularity continued. The Japanese approached him as "the only male superstar ... remaining in Shanghai." He realized they wanted to use him for propaganda purposes and made plans to escape with Wang to Hong Kong and then to Chongqing where he had been assured of more film work.[15] First, he had one more movie to make for Xinhua. The production, *Lin Chong Xue Ye Jian Chou Ji* (Lin Chong, the Outlaw), was made in an atmosphere of dread and anxiety. Lin was not an "outlaw" in reality, but he was under tremendous pressure to capitulate.

Meanwhile, a "terrorist" war between KMT agents and the Japanese puppet regime struck Shanghai between 1937 and 1941. Both sides murdered one another as well as journalists, businessmen, and politicians who were suspected of either cooperating with or resisting the Japanese. Kidnapping, theft, and crimes of all kind surged. Newspaper offices were bombed or set on fire. Zhang decided to convert Xinhua into an American company Zhongguo (China United) Pictures. He used this tactic to evade Japanese harassment as the Shanghai press had done in registering their publications as "foreign-published." It cost the studio chief a considerable fee to pay a U.S. company to be its sponsor. Zhang was praised for this action by a pro-KMT editor in Hong Kong as a "passive resister" and other newspapers as a "filmmaker with national consciousness."[16]

Sensing impending difficulties, director Wu Yonggang decided to hurry the shooting. Jin, playing Lin Chong, appearing overweight in a phony beard, wearing an elaborate official's robe, is seen training soldiers for the government. A higher court authority covets Lin's wife, Zhen Niang. After many static scenes, Lin is jailed and awaits execution by his old enemies. Thinking her husband dead, Zhen commits suicide. Lin, saved from death by a powerful monk using martial arts, vows to fight for the common people who are oppressed by the "heinous system run by cruel wolves and jackals."[17]

The story from a Song dynasty tale was adapted to conform to the strict limitations of the censors and to make use of Jin's name before he fled. Wu kept secret his knowledge that his friend was leaving. In a move, which would have made a Hollywood thriller, Jin and Wang's passage to Hong Kong was clouded with intrigue. Since both of them were well-known actors and popular celebrities, they could not just buy tickets on the night boat to the British colony. Obtaining proper documents from the Japanese would arouse suspicion. Instead, the couple went on board the steamer to say farewell to some friends at a going-away party, which was a custom at the time. In the cabin, Wang and Jin switched clothes and papers with their accomplices who probably were actor friends. When the purser shouted: "All ashore that's going ashore," the other couple descended the gang plank and disappeared into the crowd.

It was quite common for exiled film people to travel to Hong Kong. The British colony "swarmed" with them between 1937 and 1945. Many used the island as a stopping place on the way to Chongqing, Guilin, and other parts of China. Some pro-KMT filmmakers traveled back and forth between Hong Kong and Nationalist-held areas during the war.[18]

Another famous film personage, Li Lili, who had arrived in the British-held territory in 1938, welcomed Jin and Wang when they embarked. She told them that her fellow émigrés were making Mandarin-language films for the pan-Chinese market even though they were residing in a Cantonese-speaking region. Li pointed out that in some of the patriotic movies, the villains, who were Japanese collaborators, were played by Cantonese comedians whose Mandarin was awkward. Jin surmised that this technique evoked the image of Wang Jingwei, the Cantonese-speaking head of the puppet regime, which the Japanese had established in Nanjing.[19] The former vice director-general of the KMT had defected to the enemy in 1938 and formed the "Reformed National Government" in early 1940.[20]

Yet the Shanghainese were snobbish about the Hong Kongers. They felt culturally superior and believed they were bringing enlightenment to the colony. Furthermore, the mainlanders looked down on Cantonese cinema as being "trashy" and "frivolous." Famous Shanghai directors and actors, such as Cai Chusheng, Fei Mu, and Li Lili were hired by the Hong Kong branch of Chongqing-based China Film Studio to produce Mandarin films. All of this activity ceased with the Japanese takeover in December 1941. Most of the filmmakers and actors fled to safety in southwest China.[21]

Jin never stopped working. Before he could secure passage to Chongqing, Li invited him to play a role in a film she was shooting for China Central Movie Enterprises. He agreed as long as he did not have to be recognized. Wang also believed that the couple should be relatively anonymous in Hong Kong. Their goal was to find a way to travel to the area known as "Free China."

In the film, Li plays Jin Hua, "Golden Flower," a beautiful Mongolian maiden. Director Ying Yunwei was overjoyed having Jin in an unnamed part in *Sai Shang Feng Yun* (Storm on the Border). The story concerns a plot by the Japanese to instill hatred between the Mongolian and Han races. When the plan almost succeeds, Golden Flower urges her two lovers, one Han and one Mongolian, to unify the two peoples in order to defeat Japan's ambitions in the border region. At the climax, the young girl is wounded in the fighting and dies with the knowledge that her rivals are friends.[22]

Such politically charged films were now the norm. At this time, the director Sun Yu was in Chongqing developing a story about the Chinese Air Force. His aim was to show its bravery against the superior numbers of the Japanese squadrons. The director knew that Jin was to arrive soon and planned to offer him a leading role. The KMT government needed the film medium to lift the morale of its citizens since the enemy had by 1940 conquered all of the eastern part of China and was pushing westward. The film industry was now working for the same goals as the renegade Chinese government.

Traveling to Chongqing was difficult, especially from Hong Kong. Most of the heavy industries and skilled workers from Shanghai had been moved before the complete Japanese takeover of the city. They had used the Yangtze River as a means of escape —first to Hankou and then to the wartime capital in Chongqing. Others fled as far as Xian. Now the river was in enemy hands so boat travel was deemed unwise. Jin followed the only route that remained. He and Wang left by train from British Kowloon across the Chinese border and arrived in the fog-bound city after several weeks. The actor was fortunate that he was able to bring funds with him he had on deposit in Hong Kong banks. Many Shanghai citizens had kept their finances in the Crown Colony as well as in the International Settlement.[23]

Millions of Chinese also migrated to the west. Many were middle- and upper-class people who were "accustomed to wealth, power and modern amenities." There were major differences between the local provincials and the new arrivals.[24] These tensions were not reflected in the wartime films.

Sun was happy to see Jin and Wang. He described the filming problems in the beleaguered city. Unlike Shanghai, with its modern studios, Chongqing functioned with crude, underground facilities hewed out of the labyrinthine rocks of the mountain metropolis. Film stock had to be flown in from Calcutta or transported by camel or elephant over the tortuous mountain passes of the ancient caravan road from India. Everything was below the surface including cutting rooms, film processing, sound equipment, props, camera and projection rooms. From May to October all production was underground because of constant Japanese bombing. Filming moved to the surface during the winter months as the city was protected by thick layers of fog and enemy raids usually ceased.[25]

Chang Kong Wan Li (Wings of China) features Jin as Jin Wanli, a young athletic coach at Chinan Qilu University, who enlists in the Chinese Air Force. After the Japanese bomb Shanghai, Jin and his fellow pilots vow to revenge the motherland. In a dog fight over the Yangtze River, they shoot down enemy planes. One of his buddies is injured in the attack and goes to the hospital. Later the Japanese return and Jin straps himself into his airplane to pursue them. The Japanese retreat, but not before they bomb the hospital. The aviator's pal is killed. His little sister, played by Wang, also dies. As the enemy approaches again, the brave pilots take to the skies to avenge their fallen comrade.[26]

Shooting films in Chongqing was a challenge. From 1940 to 1945, only twenty features were produced and these were of poor quality. Production was hindered by the huge bureaucracy, poorly educated censors, and little financial help from the government. There was little incentive for filmmakers.[27]

Jin decided to make one more film before joining a theater troupe to perform for the troops at the front. During World War II, there were fourteen acting companies, which toured the various war zones performing for the troops. They received subsidies from the KMT Ministry of Propaganda. Many film people from Shanghai participated in the work of these groups. The themes were strictly propaganda messages. Wang Renmei also toured with her husband.[28]

Shooting scenes at the front, director Shi Dongshan used real soldiers in battle scenes which enacted a battle in Changsha. Jin enjoyed acting with local people as they portrayed the fight against the Japanese in northern Hubei. The plot of *Shengli Jinxing Qu* (Victory March) is a typical propaganda film depicting brave women and children, as well as monks, fighting the invaders to the death without surrendering.[29]

On December 8, 1941, Jin and Wang awoke in their villa on the outskirts of Chongqing, turned on their radio, and learned that the Japanese had bombed Pearl Harbor the previous day. The news also reported that twenty-four hours later the Japanese had occupied the entire International Settlement and France's Vichy government surrendered its concession. All of Shanghai was now under Japanese control. Less than two years later, Wang Jingwei's puppet regime took over the administration of the unified city.[30]

The couple remembered all of their colleagues who had chosen to remain in the so-called "orphan island" to continue filmmaking. They knew that their old boss Zhang Shankun was still making films. The movie mogul had been lucky to have Kawakita Nagamasa in charge of all cinema activities in Japanese-occupied Shanghai. He permitted the producer to continue to make entertainment films as long as there was no hint of any propaganda. The occupation's movie czar permitted Zhang to consolidate all eleven of the remaining film companies and form China United Productions in 1942. The impresario was arrested by both the Japanese and later the Chinese police during the closing days of World War II. Kawakita got him out of the Japanese prison but Zhang was jailed after he fled to unoccupied China. He later escaped to Hong Kong to begin film activities anew.[31]

Chongqing suspended all filming during the last three years of the War.[32] When the Japanese seized Hong Kong in late 1941, all studios remained closed for the duration of hostilities. Yan'an, where Mao had his headquarters, did produce a few films during this period. Edgar Snow, the American journalist, took a photo of the "Communists' First Film Studio" workers. The snapshot, however, gives the odd impression that there was no film gear available. One only sees a bunch of cold men and women bundled up in heavy quilted coats.[33]

The Communists did produce a few films, but most of them were actually movies such as *Yan'an and the Eighth Route Army* and *Dr. Bethune* about the Canadian doctor who spent the last nine months of his life with Mao's guerrilla fighters. The Shanghai intellectuals who managed to get to the CCP outpost had a difficult time adjusting to the rural, non-educated peasants. The CCP leader commented that this produced "controversies, divergences, conflicts, and discord among some of our comrades."[34]

In Chongqing, between tours, Wang and Jin invited fellow Shanghai actors to their villa. One evening Ji Tienguo, a colleague of Jin's, brought his wife, Qin Yi, to visit the couple. Qin recalled later that she was awed by the thought of meeting the "Emperor" of film. The young actress was impressed with the big villa and remembered that Wang was lively and warm, but "hardly said two words" to her. She told Ji that she admired Jin and Wang's "luxurious lifestyle." In 1944, Qin, who was to meet Jin in Shanghai after the War, heard that the couple got divorced and could not imagine they would end up parting. The youthful thespian "felt so sorry" for the pair.[35]

There are many theories concerning the reasons for the break-up of the "ideal screen couple." The war was coming to a close and tensions were increasing about the future government of China after the defeat of Japan. American forces assisting Chiang Kai-shek needed English-speaking Chinese to work for them. Wang, who had traveled to Kunming to perform in two plays, secured a job as an English typist in the Supply Department of the U.S. Army Base there.[36] Kunming was the headquarters of a training center organized by United States General Joseph Stillwell.[37] Jin was furious and forced her to quit her position. This led to many emotional scenes and arguments. Although they divorced, Jin and Wang remained friends. They had shared many happy moments in their lives. Wang continued to make films after the war and she became a colleague of Qin Yi, appearing in films with her, but never was seen with Jin on the screen again.[38]

In the spring of 1945, Germany surrendered and the war in Europe was over. It was not until August that Japan would capitulate with the allies after the United States had dropped atomic bombs on Hiroshima and Nagasaki. At the same time, the U.S.S.R. entered the war and invaded Manchuria.[39] Rivalry started between the Nationalists and the Communists to take possession of the areas occupied by the defeated Japanese. Chiang asked the United States to airlift his troops into Shanghai and other enemy-held territory so that Mao's forces could not gain access to the major metropolitan areas. The Japanese cooperated with the KMT and kept their soldiers on the streets of Shanghai until American and Nationalist forces arrived.[40]

Chiang Kai-shek's canniness in holding out for American help bore fruit. Until the end of hostilities, the Nationalist-held areas of China were demoralized. Economic production had decreased sharply, inflation was out of control, the army was ineffective and the government was corrupt.[41] Yet for most of the war, the KMT just hoarded most U.S. lend-lease supplies instead of using it against the Japanese. The CCP, on the other hand, fought the enemy in a series of guerrilla battles, which ultimately halted their advance westward. The United States tried to mediate the impending conflict between Mao and Chiang. Negotiations among Chongqing, Yan'an, and Washington continued even after the CCP and KMT forces were firing at one another in sporadic conflicts. Mao and Zhou Enlai protested the American assistance to Chiang even as they gained territory in north China and Manchuria. In a last ditch effort to avoid an all-out civil war in China, President Truman dispatched General George C. Marshall to mediate the conflict.[42] His mission failed.

Filmmakers and actors who had been away from the Hollywood of Asia during the war decided to return to Shanghai. Jin Yan, Wang Renmei, Qin Yi, and others made their way back to the liberated city by any means possible. It took Qin and an actress friend En Lu one month to return from Chongqing to Shanghai by bus.[43] Others had similar tales of endurance. The scene as the exiles approached was intimidating. Instead of Japanese warships in the harbor, American navy vessels filled the Huangpu. American soldiers were everywhere. The contrast between war-torn occupied Shanghai and the current exuberant city was remarkable.[44]

Jin Yan glanced at the river and remembered his arrival in that wonderful, horrible metropolis not quite two decades ago. Could he resume his career as the "Emperor" of film or would he be forgotten in the turmoil of post-war developments? The actor, approaching middle age, prepared himself for the challenges of 1946 and the future.

Notes

1. Wang Renmei, *Wo de cheng ming yu bu xing*, p. 278.
2. Dong, *Shanghai*, pp. 251–2.
3. Tuchman, *Stillwell and the American Experience in China*, pp. 166–7.
4. Fu Poshek, "Between Nationalism and Colonialism: Mainland Émigrés, Marginal Culture, and Hong Kong Cinema 1937–1941" in Fu and Desser (eds), *The Cinema of Hong Kong: History, Arts, Identity* (Cambridge: Cambridge University Press, 2000), p. 201.
5. Dong, op. cit., p. 256.
6. Ibid., p. 257.
7. Fu, *Between Shanghai and Hong Kong,* p. 6.
8. Fu, "Between Nationalism and Colonialism," p. 201.
9. *Encyclopedia of Chinese Films*, p. 230.
10. Wang Renmei, op. cit., pp. 166–8.
11. Ibid., pp. 193–5.
12. Fu, *Between Shanghai and Hong Kong,* pp. 48–50.
13. Ibid., pp. 26–30.
14. *Encyclopedia of Chinese Films,* pp. 227–8.
15. Fu, op. cit., p. 25.
16. Ibid., pp. 22–4.
17. *Encyclopedia of Chinese Films*, pp. 245–6.
18. Fu, op. cit., p. 52.
19. Ibid., p. 71.
20. Lloyd E. Eastman et al., *The Nationalist Era in China, 1927–1949* (Cambridge: Cambridge University Press, 1991), p. 124.
21. Fu, *Between Nationalism and Colonialism,* pp. 206–20.
22. *Encyclopedia of Chinese Films*, p. 363.
23. Eastman et al., op. cit., pp. 130–1.
24. Ibid., p. 133.
25. *New York Times*, June 14, 1942.
26. *Encyclopedia of Chinese Films*, pp. 299–300.
27. Fu, *Between Shanghai and Hong Kong,* pp. 38–40.
28. John Zao, Interview, March 1, 2007.
29. *Encyclopedia of Chinese Films*, p. 328.
30. Dong, op. cit., pp. 268–9.
31. Fu, op. cit., pp. 68–144.

32. Paul Clark, *Chinese Cinema: Culture and Politics since 1949* (Cambridge: Cambridge University Press, 1987), pp. 14–5.

33. Lois Wheeler Snow, *Edgar Snow's China* (New York: Vintage Books, 1983), p. 188.

34. Leyda, *Dianying, Electric Shadows,* pp. 151–3.

35. Qin Yi, *I Play All the Roles* (Shanghai: Shanghai Press, 1997), pp. 230–53.

36. Wang Renmei, op. cit. p. 275.

37. Tuchman, op. cit., p. 363.

38. Qin Yi, Interview, December 15, 2005.

39. Tuchman, op. cit., p. 520.

40. Dong, op. cit., p. 280.

41. Eastman et al., op. cit., p. 176.

42. Tuchman, op. cit., pp. 524–6.

43. Yao Fangzao, *Qin Yi: Shen Yuan Zhong De Mingxing* (Shanghai: Shanghai wen yi chu ban she, 1989), pp. 236–7.

44. Dong, op. cit., pp. 280–1.

CHAPTER 6

The New China

J in Yan returned to a city throttled by the KMT. He discovered that the party had taken over all of the film studios in Shanghai right after the war. They seized the excellent motion picture equipment that the Japanese had left behind. The actors and directors who had remained in the city during the occupation were accused of being "traitorous filmmakers." Many were indicted for "the crimes of conspiring with the enemy nation." A large number of them fled to Hong Kong, which benefited greatly from the talent and capital in the British colony's post-war construction.[1]

The KMT also appropriated more than 200 companies from broadcasting stations to shipping companies with no compensation given to the original owners. Government monopolies ran almost every major area of enterprise in Shanghai. Aid supplies from the United States, such as food, clothing, and medicine, were taken by Chiang and his cohorts with only a trickle reaching the poor for whom it was intended. Rampant inflation and the printing of paper money made it impossible for most of the inhabitants to survive. People just spent Chinese currency as soon as it reached their hands in order to get something of value. "To the eyes of outsiders, the Shanghainese appeared more prosperous than ever."[2] But the impression was far from the truth.

Filmmakers experienced what they had put up with before 1937. KMT censors were stricter in the 1940s than they had been in the pervious decade. Most left-wing movie people left for Hong Kong when it was obvious that they could not produce progressive films. Those who remained and had infiltrated the hostile environment of the KMT studios were called "heroes without battlefields" and "May Fourth petit-bourgeois intelligentsia" by Mao.[3]

Jin had hope of returning to the activism of the past. He sought out his friends who had returned. He shared a flat with Liu Qiong, a former basketball teammate who had become an actor. Wu Yonggang, one of Jin's favorite directors, was planning to establish a film company and told him that as soon as he organized the studio, he wanted his old star for a leading role. It had been five years since the "Emperor" performed in front of a camera. He was elated.

Liu suggested that a celebration was necessary, especially since it was the last day of the lunar year. Jin's roommate asked the actor to accompany him to the home of one of his actress friends, Qin Yi. Liu had no idea that Jin and Qin had met in Chongqing during the war nor did Jin have any recollection of the attractive young woman.

When the two men came to Qin's home, she was washing her hair, which was an old custom on New Year's Eve to begin a clean year. Someone shouted from the street below that there were a couple of guys looking for her. She propped open the window, while drying and combing her locks, and saw Jin Yan. Qin clearly remembered that she and her ex-husband had dined at the star's home in Chongqing.[4] She told them to wait in order to straighten out the room where she planned to receive her guests.

Qin wrote about the meeting in her book, *I Play All the Roles*:

> On that day, how was it that this 1930s "king of the movies"
> would come and see me? I didn't ask the reason. I was just
> thrilled. I just thought it was difficult that someone from
> my kind of family background would ever have much to
> say to him. But after we met, when he started to speak to
> us, he spoke a local dialect (he spoke Shanghainese with a
> Pudong accent). Also, he seemed to be completely at ease.
> (I believe that in the 1930s in Shanghai most of the workers
> in movies were locals from Shanghai). Due to the fact that
> we all felt intimate in our language, we soon had a sense of
> communication, there was no gap, especially when he spoke
> to my family members.[5]

Their love affair had already begun. Although the actress had
appeared in several films and was working on another one with Liu,
she considered herself unsophisticated compared with Jin. Qin felt
a little distant from the older actor and recalled that as a child she
worshipped him as an idol. It never occurred to her that she could
be friends with him. Liu arranged the initial meeting between the
two because he knew that both of them had divorced their respective
spouses during the war.

While Jin was waiting for his film work to commence, he started
to visit Qin on a regular basis. When she was not home, because
she was shooting a movie, the actor would call on her mother. They
would discuss Chinese cooking as the old lady prepared dim sum
for the handsome guest. Sometimes Jin would play mahjong with
family members. He took the game seriously saying that it was a
good way to train one's mind and improve mental skills. Qin did
not agree and told him she just could not sit still for long periods.
Jin was irritated with her restlessness and lack of concentration.

Despite the repressive political atmosphere, their romance progressed normally. The two started to meet constantly but mostly at her home. When it became obvious that they cared for one another, Jin invited Qin to go to the cinema. She was an hour late because her shooting schedule had been prolonged. Jin did not wait for her at the entrance as planned, but went inside by himself. When she arrived and found her seat he was furious. She tried to explain, but he did not pay attention. "I can't stand people who are late. Just watch the movie," he said. They viewed the film in silence and each went their separate ways after the lights went on. A few days later, Jin showed up at Qin's home with gifts. He had carved a wooden sailing ship and purchased a beautiful necklace for her. The young woman was overjoyed. She was impressed with his demeanor and thoughtfulness. Their earnest affair began with this episode.[6]

Nor did Jin's work seem seriously affected. Wu Yonggang called Jin and told him to report to the new Da Ye film studios to start shooting *Ying Chun Qu* (A Spring Melody). The actor was excited to play one of the lead parts as Dong Fangxi, a destitute painter. Dong shares a one-room flat with two other starving artists, a musician and a poet. The film was a hard-hitting exposé of life in Shanghai after the war. Scenes of bitter cold winds nipping all the leaves from Chinese parasol trees contrasted with wealthy magnates in their foreign buildings on the Bund deliriously happy about the extreme inflation opened the movie.

In the midst of the grim winter, a woman who had lost her husband and children in the war works in a Buddhist temple. After suffering many tribulations, she is accused of murder after discovering a dead man next to her one morning. The murder charges are dropped after police discover an empty bottle of amphetamines. The hopeless soul is accused of prostitution and sent to prison.

After the woman is released, she becomes ill, and looks out her window at the few remaining leaves on a parasol tree. She believes that when the last remaining leaves fall, she will die. When she awakens the next morning, she discovers the tree's foliage had disappeared but new green buds had miraculously emerged. Dong tells her she must study the strength and resolution of this tree and struggle to the bitter end. She recovers, but he becomes sick from the vapors of the wet paint in his room. The musician and the poet write an "Ode to Spring," which communicates the new season as "so bright and radiant that it is full of the power of life." The final sequence shows the people who live in the slum awaiting the arrival of spring.[7]

This not-so-subtle metaphor somehow eluded the censors. Again, as in the past, it was the outrageous melodramatic technique that made the film almost laughable to the KMT officials. Wu's extreme caricatures of the rich villains as well as the presence of Jin appeared to ease the film's acceptance.

Qin often visited the set during the shooting. She was amazed at Jin's energy preparing Korean food for the cast and crew even though he had a major role in the production. When she was working on one of her films, after the completion of *A Spring Melody*, Jin would come by to see Qin perform. He discovered that the shooting schedule for *Wu Mingshi* (Anonymous) included several late night scenes. Since the studio was located in a rough section of Shanghai, Jin suggested that she not head home alone after 2:00 a.m. Jin's flat happened to be near Qin's studio. The young actress followed her friend's advice and decided to stay the night. Their intimate relationship began.

But Jin was contemplating escape. In the summer of 1947, Jin was thinking about going to Hollywood. He explained to Qin that if he decided not to go, they could get married. However, if he made the trip, the actor realized they would have to separate. Qin was at first outraged and hurt. Later she realized that one of Jin's strongest traits was sincerity. His weakness was not being diplomatic. The couple remained together and Jin decided not to make the trip to America.

He did go to Hong Kong, though. Later that year, Qin was invited to the British colony to shoot a movie. Since Jin was not scheduled to make another film until 1948, he accompanied the rising star to the British colony. Many of Jin's old friends, colleagues, and lovers resided there. Everyday he attended banquets and enjoyed his old lifestyle. The Yong Hua Film Company offered Jin a long-term contract and also proposed a similar arrangement for Qin. She turned the proposition down because of her family in Shanghai, but urged her lover to do what he thought best for his career. He decided to return with her. Qin was happy with his response. They also made the decision to live together when they went back.

All of their friends in Hong Kong were delighted that the couple was planning to co-habit and urged them to get married. The leading artists, writers, and intellectuals, many of whom were revolutionaries, arranged a huge wedding banquet for them. Almost everyone got drunk. After the raucous ceremony and feast, the newlyweds stayed in the most expensive suite in Hong Kong's fanciest hotel. Jin almost passed out leaving the party and proceeded to vomit when he entered the bridal chamber. He then slept continuously for two days and two nights. The honeymoon was over.

Qin went back to her shooting schedule and Jin continued his rounds of partying. Five days after the wedding, the couple was invited to a banquet to honor them. In attendance were Jin's ex-wife Wang Renmei and also one of his former romantic attachments. Suddenly, after a heated conversation in Cantonese with the female guest, Jin pushed over his chair and ran out of the restaurant. The men at the table ran after him, but the former athlete was no match for them. He jumped on a tram and disappeared into the night.

Qin returned to her hotel in a daze. Was her marriage doomed? Would she see Jin again? In the early morning hours, her husband returned. Jin, full of remorse, embraced Qin and apologized. He said his actions were wrong and that he despised himself for behaving in such a manner. Qin forgave him.[8]

The confusing political atmosphere under the KMT was reflected in their relationship. The couple returned to Shanghai and lived in Jin's old flat in the southern part of the city. Qin had wanted to buy a house, but all of their savings were spent in Hong Kong.[9] Jin was able to secure a role in the film *Sheng Long Kuai Xu* (Riding the Dragon) directed by Yuan Jun. The actor stars as Situ Yan, a journalist who writes about the corruption of the society. The newspaperman returns to Shanghai from Chongqing after the war and exposes the crooked behavior of a leading family. The dishonest gang hires thugs who trash the newspaper office and beat Situ.

Wen Hui, youngest daughter of the criminal family, falls in love with the journalist. She is outraged by the actions of her kinfolk. When the public expresses support for the sister and his work, he vows to continue. The newspaper decides to open a branch office in Hangzhou. Situ, now recovered from his beating, rushes off with Wen to continue the fight in a new battleground.[10]

Now they began to experience the hardships of life in Shanghai at this time. Qin became pregnant and could not work while Jin made no films because he demanded high pay. They were running out of their meager savings. A son, Jin Jie, was born in late 1948. It was the second child for Qin who bore a daughter in her first marriage. Jin Fei Heng lived with her grandmother but took the surname of her step-father after she moved in with her mother in 1949. At the same time, Jin and Qin were offered a chance to appear in the same film. This was the first and only time they would star together in a movie.[11] Publicity was easy as both actors had fame of their own. The press, printing hints of Mao's advances against KMT forces in the civil war, looked for good news. The idea that the pair would unite on the screen as they had done in real life was received with elation by moviegoers in the inflation-riddled city.

By the end of January, all of China, north of the Yangtze, was in Communist hands. Many KMT generals had either capitulated or changed sides. Chiang resigned and his successor Li Tsung-jen tried to negotiate a peace settlement with Mao. The terms offered by the CCP were the abolishment of the KMT government, Chiang to be punished as a war criminal, and the remaining Nationalist armed forces to be integrated into the People's Liberation Army (PLA). The conditions were rejected and Mao's forces advanced southward across the Yangtze.[12] In the meantime, Chiang and hundreds of thousands of his followers fled to Taiwan. By the end of 1949, the number had reached two million.[13]

Despite the turmoil in Shanghai, filming continued at the Guo Tai Studio. *Shiqu De Aiqing* (Lost Love) was shooting as rapidly as possible. Director Tang Xiaodan cast Jin Yan as Qin Fang Qian and Qin Yi as Qiu Liyin. The plot was more daring in its depiction of KMT censorship since the city was preparing for the eventual takeover by the CCP. The lead actor is a journalist who returns to Shanghai following the war. After a brief period, the newspaper where he works is shut down because it publishes criticism of the government's suppression of the CCP rebellion. The now-unemployed writer decides to go to Hangzhou to find Qiu, his long-lost love of ten years ago.

When Qin Fang Qian finally locates the woman, he is about to knock on the door to her home when he hears Qiu's husband beating her. The former lover wants to rush in and stop the torture, but decides this would only create more trouble so he leaves. Later, he discovers what had happened in the ensuing years. When Qin Fang Qian left to fight the Japanese, his lover remained behind and soon bore their child. Later, thinking the young man had perished in the war, she married a merchant who was secretly helping the enemy. When the traitor is murdered by a maid, Qiu is accused of the crime and sentenced to death. Her lover rushes to her side on the day of the execution and is told to be brave and live on. The heavy-hearted former lover obeys her request. In the final scene, he goes to her grave to sweep it and bravely faces the future.[14]

When the shooting schedule was completed, the couple learned that late in February KMT troops had cordoned off the Bund to allow all of the gold bullion from the vaults in the Bank of China to be loaded aboard a freighter bound for Taiwan. Two months later, Nanjing fell to the PLA without a fight. Martial law was declared in Shanghai. KMT troops rounded up suspected Communists, black marketers, and other "scapegoats" for the regime's failures. Public executions at street corners without the benefit of a trial were commonplace.[15]

Many actors and filmmakers fled to Hong Kong, while others, loyal to the KMT, joined the two million Nationalists by the end of the year in Taiwan. Jin and Qin had to decide. Many of their close friends picked the British Colony. The couple knew that they could obtain filming engagements there. Their decision was easy. Qin Yi planned to join the CCP. Jin Yan, while not a party member, was dedicated to the idea that he could contribute to the building of a new China. Both had participated in films that were progressive in nature and critical of the status quo. The two believed they could apply their talents in assisting the new nation that was not far off.

On May 24, Nationalist forces evaporated. Most had fled or exchanged their uniforms for black gowns and melted into the crowds. Around midnight, Mao's peasant soldiers entered Shanghai through the former French concession in an orderly manner. When the city awakened the next morning, the PLA was in control.[16] Instead of forcing themselves into people's homes as the KMT armies had done, the Communist troops declined use of beds saying they did not want to impose on the public and slept on the streets of the metropolis.[17]

Two worlds came into conflict when Shanghai was liberated by the CCP: one was the entrepreneurial out-looking spirit of Chinese modernization and the other was the world of peasant simplicity and revolutionary ardor "fuelled by a desire for revenge."[18] The long Civil War between Chiang and Mao had been a struggle between an exhausted ineffective government and "a communist movement whose control over the countryside made it all but indestructible."[19]

Calm returned to Shanghai. *Lost Love* was released to movie theaters. The film only screened for a short period because of the changing situation. Theater owners, unsure of the political climate, were worried about the content of the movie. A few critics had implied that there had been "subtle sentiments" in the story.[20]

For Qin Yi and Jin Yan, however, the transition was smooth enough. She was honored by the new administration as one of the "Top Four Actresses in China."[21] Qin was asked by the CCP to assist in the planning of the Shanghai Movie Company. The party-run studio projected a series of films which could heal pre-Liberation wounds with a forward-looking emphasis on the need for both individual effort and team work.[22]

Both actors were asked to join the new company and were put on a regular salary. Jin received more than Qin, but their income was much higher than average. The CCP gave them a luxurious and beautiful six-room apartment in the quiet West District. Qin invited her mother and sister to join her two children and husband in the spacious flat.[23]

Jin, while not involved in a production, continued drinking which he had always done before. The actor tried to restrain himself during the day when he was taking care of Jin Jie, while the boy's mother would be working at the studio preparing for her various roles.

In September, a Political Consultative Conference was held with 662 delegates from the CCP, Democratic League, other "democratic groups," and representatives from labor, peasants, and business and industry. The body adopted the Common Program of the People's Republic of China and designated Beijing as the official capital. On October 1, Mao officially proclaimed the founding of the People's Republic of China.[24]

Jin and Qin stayed up all night and joined the millions of Shanghainese on the streets celebrating the historic occasion. Fireworks illuminated the skies over the Bund. People were singing and dancing in the streets. A feeling of joy and anticipation for the future of the New China permeated their hearts.

Notes

1. Fu, *Between Shanghai and Hong Kong*, pp. 135–40.
2. Dong, *Shanghai*, pp. 284–5.
3. Clark, *Chinese Cinema*, pp. 5–19.
4. Yao, *Qin Yi*, pp. 248–52.
5. Qin, *I Play All the Roles*.
6. Ibid.
7. *Encyclopedia of Chinese Films*, pp. 401–2.
8. Qin, op. cit.
9. Yao, op. cit., p. 261.
10. *Encyclopedia of Chinese Films*, p. 407.
11. Yao, op. cit., pp. 261–2.
12. Eastman et al., *The Nationalist Era in China*, pp. 346–51.

13. R. R. C. de Crespigny, *China This Century* (Sydney: Thomas Nelson (Australia) LTD, 1975), p. 176.

14. *Encyclopedia of Chinese Films*, p. 465.

15. Dong, op. cit., pp. 290–2.

16. Ibid., p. 293.

17. Snow, *Edgar Snow's China*, p. 264.

18. Graham Hutchings, *Modern China: A Guide to a Century of Change* (Cambridge, MA: Harvard University Press, 2001), p. 376.

19. Ibid., p. 9.

20. Cho, *Blooming Flower in Shanghai*, p. 118.

21. *Shanghai Star*, March 27, 2003.

22. Tony Rayns and Scott Meek (eds), *Electric Shadows: 45 Years of Chinese Cinema* (London: BFI, Dossier No. 3, 1980), p. E8.

23. Yao, op. cit., p. 263.

24. Eastman et al., op. cit., pp. 351–3.

CHAPTER 7

Sick and Alone

The Shanghai Movie Company started production soon after the formal establishment of the People's Republic of China. Although Qin Yi, and to some degree Jin Yan, had been involved in the planning of the CCP production studio, tension developed between their Shanghai culture and those who had arrived from Yan'an, the Communist base area during the civil war. This unease between the two forces would pervade and dominate filmmaking for many years. The Shanghai moviemakers were associated with the social and geographical elements that had the least trust of the CCP leadership. The cadres from the countryside had views and backgrounds quite different from the experienced filmmakers.[1]

One of the challenges the old-time leftist movie people faced was that they no longer were infiltrating the KMT system but now worked in a nationalized industry. Instead of appealing to urban dwellers, they now had to reach out to the rural, less educated population. These veterans had to change their mode of operation.[2] In addition, the CCP established two other production facilities for film, the former Japanese studios in Changchun and one in Beijing staffed with former Yan'an personnel.[3]

Political activism against the government seemed no longer necessary. The first year of the PRC was very successful. The so-called "New Democracy" spawned land reform and a fresh Marriage Law. The government's campaign against the bourgeoisie created new commonalities and identities.[4] Their policy was to include almost everyone except "enemies of the people" such as big landlords and bureaucratic capitalists who had held large enterprises and had been connected to the KMT.[5]

Jin was pleased that he got a featured part in *Da Di Chong Guang* (The Return of Spring) directed by Xu Tao. He had wanted the lead role of the commander of the New Fourth Army who attempts to follow the armistice agreement between the CCP and the KMT that was signed after the surrender of Japan in 1945. However, Jin's part of Old Shen, the machine-gunner, provided the actor with an opportunity to demonstrate his cooperation with the new studio leaders.

The plot of *The Return of Spring* has the KMT forces violating the armistice and the PLA soldiers are forced to retreat. Old Shen, the commander and a medic, remain behind in order to help the wounded. They are captured by the enemy following a battle but escape after killing the KMT leader. The three return to their unit where the fighting against their foe continues. Waging a guerrilla war, the PLA becomes stronger and stronger. By 1949, the troops cross the Yangtze and advance southward. The last scene shows a guerrilla team joining the PLA to final victory.[6] Jin proved he knew how to handle weapons. The actor not only fired rounds in his machine gun, but assisted some of the other cast in dealing with their rifles. The film was released in 1950.

But Jin was no longer valued as a movie icon. The studio was planning to make a film about the peasant rebellion during the Qing dynasty. Jin had his sights set on playing the part of Jingshi Song, the revolt's leader. He was not selected by the movie's director. The actor was crushed and felt defeated. He had initially believed that after the revolution, he would have greater chances to star in films.[7] On the other hand, Jin was picked to be the head of the Actors' Guild and devoted himself to helping the younger performers perfect their skills. In addition, his job required that he administer many details of the actors' activities.

Qin Yi, on the other hand, kept getting chosen for many film roles and soon became one of China's most popular stars. The couple often was so busy and many times in two different places that they did not see one another for weeks at a time. In the spring of 1951, Jin was sent to Beijing to represent model workers in a national conference. He wrote Qin a letter, the first since their love affair began, about the great honor he had received in the capital. Jin was awarded a plaque as an exemplary worker. She was overjoyed to think he had faith in the party and replied that she now felt a new sense of intimacy again. That exchange of letters was the only correspondence the two would share for their whole lives.[8]

But new threats emerged. Later that year and into 1952, the Rectification Movement started. Jin was accused of having habits like growing flowers, raising birds and dogs, and other bourgeoisie hobbies. The actor tried to defend himself but that only caused more accusations against him. Qin persuaded him to give up those endeavors. Jin did not agree with her but really had no choice. He was not happy and began to drink again. He also started to have an affair with a female co-worker. Since Qin was extremely busy with her film schedule and shooting on location, she did not discover the details until much later.[9]

When Qin finally learned about Jin's infidelity, she was pregnant with their second child. She was contemplating an abortion, but could not summon the courage to make the decision. Her pregnancy was marred by the conflict with her husband. The couple decided to sleep in separate rooms. Jin slept in the living room.

After almost eight years of marriage, Qin did not want it to end. She could ill afford the scandal of a divorce. She hoped no one would discover that they were separated, albeit in their own home. One night, after a fight, Jin left the apartment and went out to drink. A fellow worker escorted him back home well after midnight. Qin realized that the entire studio would find out. The next day, everyone at the Shanghai Movie Company learned the truth. At this point, Qin thought about dissolving the marriage, but listened to a party leader who suggested that she talk with Jin and try to resolve the matter. Her husband refused to discuss it with her.[10]

They might as well have been divorced, for all the intimacy that remained in their union was a façade. Qin's labor started in the middle of the night and she went to the hospital in a hired three-wheeled cart all alone. She did not awaken Jin. The child was stillborn. In the morning, she called and asked him to come to the hospital. Jin said he could not respond to her request because he was taking a political test that day. He told her that if he did not appear at the exam, people would think he was skipping the test and that would be a real loss of face. Jin said even if one took the test and did poorly, that would be okay. Qin respected his decision and Jin did call in the afternoon to ask about her condition and to report that he had passed. She never forgot this incident but remained calm, kept her anger down, and rested at the hospital for a week. The doctor remarked that he was impressed she was able to have painless postpartum.[11] Jin did visit her during her stay there but did not accompany her home. She left the hospital as she had come, alone. Qin did not want others to know the truth, so she told everyone that Jin was too busy to help.[12]

While Jin and Qin were having marital problems, their nation was undergoing vast changes. All private enterprises were nationalized and the CCP consolidated its power by adopting a formal constitution. The National People's Congress (NPC) was established.[13] In the film world, all motion pictures made had to be approved by the Film Bureau. The government established film projection teams that traveled throughout the countryside. By 1955, there were 2,300 units. They played a significant part in increasing the audiences for film.

During the early 1950s, filmmakers were told to repudiate the Shanghai heritage. During and after the Korean War, all American films were eliminated and Soviet and socialist bloc productions were substituted. The ideologues from Yan'an were now in charge. Older Shanghai movie veterans "were expected to undertake ideological remolding, but they also had the skills essential to the growth of the industry." Inexperienced artists as well as Yan'an trained cadres were assigned to work with these senior people, which the latter did not relish. To further dismiss the heritage of Shanghai, the government established film production centers in the interior to decentralize and to make the former Hollywood of Asia less dominant in the industry.[14]

Qin Yi was accepted for membership in the Communist Party, which by the 1950s was not as easy to join as before. The CCP tried "to maintain quality control of its new members." Mao believed that one of the reasons the KMT failed was that they accepted almost anyone who wanted to join. During its first decade in power, the CCP screened out "the carriers of the old political culture." The party grew from a membership of 1.2 million in 1945, to 5.8 million by 1950, and 17 million by 1961.[15] Jin Yan chose not to join. Qin Yi believed the reason he made that decision is because everything he did he wanted to give 100 percent and be perfect. He felt that he just could not do that.[16] Jin must have been bitter about his fall from stardom under the party's ascendancy. The former left-wing progressive was not in sync with the pronouncements of the cadres from Yan'an.

Eventually, the party studio asked Jin to play the role of the minister of industry in *Wei Da De Qi Dian* (The Great Beginning) directed by Zhang Ke. The actor was delighted to be reunited with his old friend from Lianhua days, Xuang Shaofen, who did the cinematography. The story, filmed in 1954, was a foreshadowing of the Great Leap Forward, Mao's ill-fated plan to increase production in China. In the movie, a big steel mill reacts to Chairman Mao's call to improve the production and minimize the waste. The new head of the steel-making department, with support from the CCP secretary, suggests upgrading the factory's fifteen-ton steel-making furnace to a twenty-ton one so the mill can make 5,000–6,000 extra tons of steel for the country. Many workers endorse the plan, but conservative officials and the factory director oppose the suggestion. The opposition represents self-complacency from past working experience. They believe it is risky to upgrade the furnace.

In the film, the CCP secretary is elected by the workers to meet with the minister of industry to seek his help. Encouragement for the upgrade is given by the official and the installation's first try meets with failure. The conservatives at the plant say again that it was a bad idea. However, the workers check every detail and discover that the system is okay but that they had overused gas the first time. The problem is solved and the factory breaks previous records of producing steel. A superimposition on the screen proclaims: "This is a great beginning of the ever-lasting battle of the working class to fulfill the goal of industrialization of the communist country."[17]

Jin played the role of the minister with great dignity. Instead of what could have been a cardboard character, his interpretation of the official was natural and warm. The actor was rewarded with an important part in *Mu Qin* (Mother). He plays Old Deng, a Communist leader in the 1930s. Director Ling Ziefeng uses the film as a history of the CCP. Zhang Ruifang, who stars as the mother, was assisted in her acting technique by Jin. The veteran guided the actress as she aged from the 1920s until the founding of the PRC.[18]

Old Deng helps the mother and her family to survive in hard times. He educates them about the CCP and her son joins the party. When the mother observes her husband's death at the hands of a cruel supervisor, she understands why Old Deng continues his work planning the revolution. She vows to help the CCP and operates with him when the party goes underground after the Shanghai massacre. The mother joins the CCP and then Old Deng and the son are betrayed by a traitor and arrested. Old Deng is executed.

Later in the film, the son is released from prison. Mother and son fight the Japanese as guerrillas, but she is captured and imprisoned. After the war, she gets out and continues to help the CCP as a secret agent posing as a cigarette peddler. The mother provides the PLA with intelligence so their army can attack and liberate the city. After victory, she is reunited with her son.[19]

While the plot sounds like the same old propaganda piece, the film is shot Soviet-style in a social-realism technique. The story is a loose adaptation of Gorky's *Mother*. There are many lap dissolves and the acting is brilliant. Jin's manner and hair appeared to be similar to that of Chairman Mao's. The character of the mother symbolized the CCP and its revolution. She endured every hardship imaginable and achieved final victory over the forces of capitalism and imperialism.

But this was a far cry from his heyday as the "Emperor" of film. In between films, Jin continued his drinking. While shooting however, he abstained from alcohol. He smoked countless cigarettes as did most Chinese. The actor refrained from criticizing publicly certain party leaders during "The Hundred Flowers" thaw of 1957. Others were not so smart. When the brief period encouraging examination of party ways ended, the complainers were attacked as "rightists." Most of the Shanghai filmmakers and their faults were emphasized in the Anti-Rightist Campaign that followed.[20]

Both Jin and Qin continued to work. The actress had lead roles in two of the most popular films during this period, *Woman Basketball Player Number 5* and *Guerrillas on the Railway.*[21] Youthful idealism was the common theme of these movies as well as many others produced.[22]

Filmmaking was now pure propaganda. But Jin was still able to exploit his natural talents. The Changchun studio in Manchuria had plans to make a film about loyal Tibetans. Sun Yu, who had been selected to play Huo Wa, a PLA hero from the 1930s, suggested to director Wang Yi that Jin Yan would be fantastic in the role of Lao Ba'er, an old Tibetan hunter. Jin, thrilled to be part of a production with his former mentor, hurried quickly to the northern location.

Bao Feng Yu Zhong De Xiong Ying (Eagles Brave the Storm) was shot in wild territory mostly in Tibet. Jin, in one of the leads, is dynamic as he plays a hardy outdoorsman riding on horseback wearing sheepskin. Lao helps Red Army soldiers who had escaped after being captured by Nationalist forces. He feeds and houses them in his tent. The local Tibetans want to turn over the men to the KMT government. Lao is about to release them when enemy troops arrive. The old hunter helps them to kill the invaders.

Huo Wa, one of the PLA men, wants to rescue his commander who is still in captivity. Lao and his son escort him to enemy territory where they free the commander late at night. Lao's son is captured and the commander offers to exchange himself for the young man. Instead, the PLA and local people attack the enemy and rescue the son. The commander is wounded and orders the men to retreat. Instead, they ask Huo to take the mortally injured officer and escape with the Tibetans. The Red Soldiers fight to the death allowing the others to make it to the Yellow River. The commander dies, but before the Tibetans cross over to safety, they bury the PLA officer. They remark that a Red Army soldier shed his last drop of blood for the Tibetans.[23]

Conditions on location for *Eagles Brave the Storm* were horrible. The cast lived in tents and ate lamb and bear meat. Sometimes they had to have their food uncooked. It was windy and quite cold. Often it snowed. Jin drank huge quantities of Chinese wine as well as the local brew, both of which had high alcohol content. When the film was completed, the studio was very pleased with the results, but Jin started to suffer from extreme stomach pains.

In 1958, the actor got a rare opportunity to shoot a movie in the German Democratic Republic. Qin Yi was excited and thought that this opportunity could help her husband turn his life around. She believed it could be similar to the experience he had at the model worker conference held in Beijing several years before.

Jin was happy that he had been selected to represent China at the Berlin studios. He planned his outfits with great care and studied German as well as reviewing his English. He told Qin that as a representative of his country he should have his own dignity. She assured him that she knew with his acting skills and personal deportment he would not lose face for the PRC.

The script for the international film underwent several revisions. The shooting was delayed for two months. Jin was having terrible stomach problems but participated in many meetings with the director. Production was suspended and the foreign actors were furloughed. Before Jin departed for China, he went to the East German department store to buy medicine accompanied by the film's director and his assistant. He used his per diem money to purchase a tape recorder to use to learn his lines better. The director told him not to spend his own money. It should be a gift from the film company. Jin refused but his host insisted. He finally relented and took the men out for dinner to say goodbye for the moment.

Jin had no way of knowing that the acceptance of the gift would end up as charges against him. Someone at the Chinese Embassy in Berlin wrote a report about him. A letter with the accusations was handed to the actor to take back with him and give to the Ministry of Culture. He did not know its contents when he delivered the document to the Ministry when he returned to Beijing.

Later that same day, Jin fainted in the bathroom of his hotel. He was taken to the hospital and diagnosed with bleeding ulcers and total exhaustion. His trip to Europe included a lot of travel to many countries of the Eastern bloc, while waiting for the film to commence shooting. The hospital phoned Qin and notified her that her husband was seriously ill and to come at once. Jin called her the next day just before she was to depart for the airport. He told her not to come; he was returning to Shanghai.

Arriving home on a stretcher, Qin took him to the hospital. He explained that he knew she could not take care of him in Beijing and she agreed. From that time on, Jin never regained his health. He recovered enough to make two final films.[24]

Although Jin was not feeling like his old self, he forced himself to continue working. He wanted to participate in Mao's new idea, the Great Leap Forward. Since the PRC's first Five-Year Plan (1953–1957) was successful, with the GNP increasing 9 percent on average each year, the Chairman set a goal of "doubling output." All sectors of the economy were to be involved.[25]

The film industry was included in the movement along with agriculture, steel and coal, all major enterprises, and even "backyard furnaces." The government established even more studios, this time in smaller cities. Film production for the entire nation increased from 82 features in 1956–1957 to 187 in 1958–1959.[26] Many movies were shot quickly and were poor quality. It is estimated that more were produced than actually recorded.

Factories and agricultural communes gave false results to Beijing. The government-controlled newspapers announced achievements each day and the public was exhorted to produce more and more. In 1958, for example, steel production was eight million tons, short of the eleven-million-ton goal but three million tons of steel was unusable, having been made in the so-called "backyard furnaces." It was the same problem in agriculture.[27]

Jin's last screen appearances were emblematic of the Great Leap Forward. *Hai Shang Hong Qi* (Red Flag over the Sea) is a wonderful example of this genre. Sailors return in their ship, the 500-ton *Peace*, to Shanghai for repairs. They decide to undertake the labor themselves so that the workers at the shipyard will have time to build more new vessels. A British ship anchors alongside and its captain ridicules the seamen's attempts. The Chinese first mate discovers that the westerner's ship will be sailing for London in three days. Party members, sailors, workers and their families work day and night to prepare the *Peace* for the sea. Party Secretary Tang, played by Jin, joins the ship as it heads out to journey with the British ship, which is twice as large. At first, the foreign vessel keeps ahead in the competition and the Chinese crew is very nervous. Later under the leadership and support of Secretary Tang and the first mate, the sailors tighten the safety valves, and enhance their speed. The *Peace* finally catches up with and then steams ahead of the western ship.[28]

The second feature produced with Jin during this period was *Ai Chang Ru Jia* (Love the Factory as Your Home). The plot is similar to so many films made at the time. A factory in Shanghai manufacturing goods for many industries cannot meet the demands of its customers who are under pressure to meet the goals of the Great Leap Forward. The plant head and the employees try to find a technological breakthrough to enhance production to meet the market demand. An old-time worker is against the plan. The first test fails and they are requested to abandon the experiment. The district industry director, played by Jin, supports the plant head and the reason for the initial failure is discovered. This development allows the construction of more factory buildings and workers' dorms.

At the same time, the veteran worker understands his error and leads the campaign to save material as part of the anti-waste movement. The factory now sets up a higher goal of production trying to challenge a ship-building factory that has been established for over one hundred years.[29]

Jin, by the close of 1958, was just too tired to work in any more films. After appearing in almost forty features, he was too weak to continue. The actor stayed at home caring for his retarded boy and spending time with his step-daughter who he treated as his own blood. Qin was away most of the time on shoots. When she was at the apartment, they continued to sleep in separate rooms. She was not pleased with the way Jin disciplined his son Jin Jie, but relented when she saw him bathe and teach him games to improve his I.Q. The actor purchased a set of imported tools and began to craft objects out of wood and other materials. His training in architectural skills at Nankai provided the impetus for development of the talent to use his hands with dexterity.[30]

Jin used the time at home to improve his cooking, carve toys for his children, knit sweaters, grow flowers, perfect his English, and interact with his son and daughter. His daughter, Jin Fei Heng, recalled that her father was serious about everything he did. "He was extremely capable and could do anything."[31]

Even though Jin was ill with stomach ulcers, he would sometimes go to the studio and do work on his own. If there was anything wrong, he would fix it. Once, the electric light in the ping-pong room in the great hall was broken. He immediately climbed up and repaired it. A new, young actor who had just joined the company thought he was a handyman and had no idea he was the leader of the Actor's Guild.[32]

Jin watched sports on television at home but despite the pain in his stomach, he continued to participate in limited physical activity. He taught Jin Jie tai chi, ping pong, and badminton. He designed a sweater with a thumbhole in the sleeve so he could write in cold weather and then proceeded to knit the garment. His home-made kimchi was famous. All of his friends and colleagues wanted to have some mixed with their rice. Many of his visitors were renowned painters and Jin enjoyed showing them his drawings, which he continued to create after his health deteriorated even more.[33]

Although Jin could not play basketball any longer, he was the driving force in starting a team at the film company. As a former superb athlete, he now viewed every sports broadcast on China Central TV. He also watched the news and then reported the contents to the family each night. The standing joke in the household was that if anyone wanted to know the weather, they could just ask father. He was never jealous of Qin's success in films. In fact, he encouraged her several times to seek certain roles because of her talent.[34]

The political life of the nation was also in turmoil. The Great Leap Forward was a disaster. Over thirty million Chinese were wiped out by famine between 1959 and 1962.[35] Grain production had been exaggerated to be from 375 million to 500 million tons. By 1959, the party started to relax the policies of the Great Leap Forward. Premier Zhou Enlai played a key role in initiating the recovery process, which was extended until 1965.[36]

Thanks to Zhou, Chinese cinema made progress in the late 1950s and early 1960s. The film industry was attacked by both the right and left elements of the party. Xia Yan, minister of film culture, wrote: "Zhou encouraged us to turn our backs on these cares and concentrate on our work."[37]

Jin avoided the struggles in 1961 between the peasants of the CCP and its urban bureaucratic members. Mao then instituted a "Socialist Education Campaign" to reemphasize the class struggle. Work teams were organized to live with the peasants to expose "backsliding" among local leadership. Those brigades were a precursor to the Cultural Revolution.[38]

Another reason Jin did not appear in any more films is that he might not have been asked. It was common knowledge that the actor was not impressed with the direction that Chinese cinema was heading. The film styles in the PRC between 1956 and 1964 had four features: the typical characters and events of past centuries had relevance to the concerns and people of the present; heroes and heroines were presented with glossiness and glamour avoiding naturalism and critical realism (which was the opposite of Jin Yan's style of naturalistic acting); the emphasis was placed on writer and script, not director; and, there was an extended use of dialogue and stage-derived presentations.[39]

On the other hand, Jin may have removed himself from playing in these films, which were filled with caricatures. Enemies were one-dimensional; foreigners were never portrayed realistically; and, there was little character development among both positive and negative actors. The movies borrowed from the stage and broke away from Soviet socialist realism.[40] This latter development was not surprising since China broke its ties with the U.S.S.R. and all Russian technicians were ordered to leave.[41] In addition, Jin, who had been influenced by the May Fourth writers, found that their heroes and heroines were prettified and the stories had been simplified because the party cadres thought the people would not understand their original complexity. Jin could not believe that audiences that had no difficulty with the rapid transitions of time and space in Chinese opera were deemed by the Yan'an clique to find these passages incomprehensible in film. He found that many artists and cadres seemed to have shared this underestimation of the masses.[42]

In late 1962, Jin started to bleed at home and was rushed to the hospital. The doctor on duty removed his stomach, which resulted in making him even more tired and unable to eat much food at one sitting. He had to lie down for at least two hours after each meal.[43] Since Qin was busy shooting all day, Jin Fei Heng took care of her father and brother. She served him snacks and ran errands for him. His daughter accompanied him to the hospital on many occasions for check-ups. She worshipped her father and overlooked his bad moods caused by the illness.[44]

Outside, things were going from bad to worse. Some CCP leaders blamed Mao for the failure of the Great Leap Forward and proceeded to rule China without seeking his approval. In 1966, the Chairman struck back at the bureaucrats. He swam across the Yangtze River accompanied by hundreds of young people. The following month, Mao wrote a wall poster denouncing Deng Xiaoping and others. Millions of youth came to Beijing to parade in front of the Chairman. Mao's intent was to use these Red Guards to exert pressure on the educational and party bureaucracies. This new political campaign came to be known as the "Great Proletarian Cultural Revolution."[45]

Mao's partners were the so-called "Gang of Four": Jiang Qing, the Chairman's wife and former second-rate film star from Shanghai; Zhang Chunqiao; Yao Wenyuan; and Wong Hongwen.[46] The PLA, controlled by Lin Biao, allowed the Red Guards to seize government headquarters in Beijing.[47]

Anarchy and violence ruled. Party officials were humiliated in public and paraded through the streets in dunce caps. Teachers, intellectuals, artists, and filmmakers were killed or committed suicide. Their libraries and apartments were vandalized. Anyone interested in western music or culture was criticized. Hobbies such as fishing, stamp collecting, growing flowers, keeping pet birds, cats, or dogs were condemned as petty bourgeoisie amusements. The Cultural Revolution interfered in the daily lives of everyone.[48]

Shanghai and other cities of China had their own Red Guard attacks. Jin could look out of his window and see the teenagers with red armbands marching in the street holding aloft in their hands *The Quotations of Chairman Mao*. One day, when he was home alone with Jin Jie, a group of wild youngsters in their early teens knocked on the door. Jin's retarded son opened it, while his father was lying down. The mob pushed the boy aside and observed the books in the apartment. They began to tear pages from them and Jin Jie tried to stop them and started to have a tantrum. Not knowing he was having a panic attack, the ruffians knocked the boy down. Jin came out of his room and ordered them to leave at once. As he tried to pick his son up, the Red Guards fled. Jin Jie never recovered completely from the traumatic experience. Jin Yan realized that his hobbies had to be curtailed. He did hide his tool box and some of his drawings in case the thugs returned.

When Qin returned home, she was horrified. She told her husband that all production at the studio had ceased and that the minister of film culture, their old colleague from Shanghai, Xia Yan, had been vilified and denounced. He lost his job, but later continued to write screenplays and essays.[49]

Events deteriorated even more as the Cultural Revolution progressed. Madame Mao was put in charge of all cultural and artistic activities, including film. She and the rest of the "Gang of Four" made the cinema one of the chief scapegoats in their seizure of power and began persecuting the rank-and-file film workers. Even Zhou's favorite motion pictures were branded "poisonous weeds."[50] During this first year of anarchy, all production ceased. The film industry's most experienced workers were removed from their posts; many of them were broken physically or mentally in the course of their re-education.[51] The Cultural Revolution was the nadir for the artists, writers, and filmmakers from 1930s Shanghai and post-World War II. It is estimated that thirty or more former Shanghai movie people died under attack during this period.[52]

All over China, schools were closed, factories shut down, and Red Guards roamed the streets creating havoc. Finally, Mao had to ask Lin Biao to have the PLA restore order. The "Gang of Four" had representatives at all of the film studios. Their role was to decide who to send to the countryside or to work in factories. Those banished were accused of being "capitalist roaders."[53] Jin Yan and Qin Yi were no exceptions. Jin was the more fortunate of the pair. He was "sent down" to a cadre school for one year to do general handyman's work, while Qin was exiled from her home for four years. She was confined for the first year in a correctional institution and the remaining time was spent on a farm.[54]

At one time in their banishment, they were on the same farm and separated by a wall. They had no knowledge that the other person was there. The couple discovered the fact only afterwards. Jin returned to Shanghai after a year as his health was so bad that the cadres sent him home. Qin had to wait another three years before her release.

The Shanghai that Jin knew before the Cultural Revolution did not exist when he came back. His film studio was in the hands of the Yan'an clique. They had seized control of the propaganda apparatus in the city. Their cultural influence was even greater than during the Anti-Rightist Campaign. They rejected cosmopolitanism and advocated a modified Chinese operatic tradition.[55] By the time Qin returned, limited film production started up again.

But it would never be the same again. In 1970, Jiang Qing devised a new type of Beijing opera that could be made into a film. *The Red Lantern* was the first feature to be made since the silencing of the studios four years before. The theme of the movie was based on Mao's stricture that: "after the armed enemies have been eliminated, the unarmed enemies still survive. We must struggle with them to death; we should not take these enemies lightly."[56] Only a few features and several documentaries were made during the next few years. Many of these productions continued to carry this message. Madame Mao carried on exerting total power and authority over the arts.[57]

While the studios were open, little filming was done. The actors and directors participated in endless discussions. Passivity was the chosen technique to keep out of trouble since the cadres in charge were not consistent in their views. Jay Leyda in his research found these words of advice, which were the "private program of the Chinese film industry":

> ...we should always make the effort to contribute to the discussion in these [political] meetings, but we should not be the first to speak. We should not be the last either [though it usually worked out this way for films]; a place in the middle was best. Also, we should not speak for too long a time, or for too short a time. [In films, be careful not to be too long-winded or too abrupt.] Again, a median approach was the

> best. Above all, we should never, under any circumstances,
> introduce a new idea. We should only repeat the ideas that had
> been expressed by those who had spoken first. We should not
> be original even in our phraseology; we should express the
> same ideas in the same words that had been used before.[58]

It is difficult to discover what really went on in the Shanghai
Movie Company during this period. Yomi Braester, the noted
Chinese film scholar, uses an essay by Zhang Xianliang to dramatize
the difficulties of keeping a truthful record during the Cultural
Revolution. "Zhang tells how, in 1971, he destroyed the only
photograph of his father, because it would have incriminated him
as a capitalist."[59]

When Jin and Qin finally were able to return to their apartment,
she discovered that her mother had died and their daughter had been
spared being "sent-down." The young woman found a job at a silk
export business and continued to take care of her brother. Jin Fei
Heng also had been chosen to be the secretary at various criticism
meetings.[60] Jin Yan continued to sleep in a separate room, but Qin
still prepared small exquisite breakfasts for her husband. When she
was home from the studio, she made Jin a three-dish lunch. One time,
during one of his bad moods, he demanded egg noodles in a bowl.
His wife complied, but complained to a reporter: "He always tortures
me like this!"[61] Yet, the couple stayed together and discussed movies
and the weather. They did not talk about their experiences when they
were in exile. Years later, Qin remarked that their problems during
the Cultural Revolution were so much less than others'.[62]

Zhou Enlai, who had remained as premier, assisted in easing the
harshness of the past six years. He met secretly with Henry Kissinger,
U.S. President Richard Nixon's national security advisor, in 1971, to
prepare for an historic encounter between Nixon and Chairman Mao
the following winter. These talks resulted in American recognition

of the PRC and the breaking of diplomatic relations with Chiang Kai-shek on Taiwan.[63]

A year later, as conditions improved, Mao and Zhou presided over a government that was "an uneasy balance of left and right." The former was xenophobic and the latter advocated broader diplomatic and trade ties with non-Communist nations. The premier's side was becoming more influential when Zhou died in January 1976. A mass sentiment of mourning enveloped the Chinese nation. Then in September, Mao died.[64] The "Gang of Four" was arrested under instructions from Hua Guofeng, the Chairman's successor.

Jiang Qing's incarceration meant that filmmakers could challenge the prevailing totalitarian aesthetics.[65] Qin Yi returned to full-time work at the studio and her colleagues were involved in an increased number of productions. The Rightists were rehabilitated and restored to positions of influence.[66] By 1978, Deng reestablished his power behind the scenes.[67] Mistakes made during the Cultural Revolution were recognized. Production of Western-style feature films resumed and the Beijing Film Academy was reopened.[68]

Unfortunately, Jin Yan could not take advantage of this "Second Hundred Flowers" period.[69] In addition to his botched operation, which prevented him from eating properly, he developed emphysema. Every day he coughed and gasped. Anyone who saw him in this condition believed he was dying. Jin now had to spend weeks at a time in the hospital where he could receive proper treatment with oxygen and medicine. Since Qin was shooting films on many occasions, the actor found himself alone countless days. Even when he was at home, he had to rest in bed most of the time. The former athlete summoned enough energy to take care of the flowers he had planted on the balcony. As the illness progressed, one pot after another withered. He managed to drag himself to the last white flower standing alone and continued to water it.

Qin continued to make breakfast for him before she left for work. She left food for the weakened actor, but he could barely eat. His wife tried to cheer him up with news that foreign films from Romania, North Korea, Japan, and even the United States were being shown again in cinema theaters. Charlie Chaplin's *Modern Times* played to packed houses.[70] Pre–Cultural Revolution films including Qin's were screened. There are no records that indicate Jin's Shanghai films were ever exhibited again.

Things were changing too fast. By the early 1980s, Deng's philosophy that "there can be no communism with pauperism, or socialism with pauperism. So, to get rich is not a sin" was being put into practice.[71] The new paramount leader started the "Four Modernizations" Campaign, which enabled the film industry to develop new plans for increased production. As the prime mass communication medium in the country, the cinema mirrored the changing circumstances and also played a vital part in reshaping the society.[72] Jin, hospitalized for months in 1983, could not participate in the renaissance of his beloved profession.

In late December 1983, Qin was shooting the film *Thunder Storm*. She received a call from the hospital that Jin was in critical condition. She thought he would get better and be able to return home as he did in past years. But this time, the frail former movie star was far too sick to recover. Qin was at his bedside for four days. According to author Yao Fan, during the last thirty hours of Jin's life, she did not leave him alone "for even one second." She felt that no one was good enough to take care of her husband. As Jin's breathing became fainter, he opened his eyes widely and tears streamed down his face. He looked into Qin's eyes with feelings of shame, pain, and guilt.[73]

Jin's wife of thirty-six years gazed back into the eyes of her husband. She too communicated regret. Qin blamed herself for not being able to spend more time with him, especially the last ten years. For a decade, the old Rudolph Valentino of Shanghai had been sick and alone. He died on December 27, 1983 at the age of seventy-three.[74] Now all that remained was his memory.

Notes

1. Clark, *Chinese Cinema*, pp. 2–3.
2. Ibid., p. 20.
3. Ibid., pp. 30–2.
4. R. Keith Schoppa, *The Columbia Guide to Modern Chinese History* (New York: Columbia University Press, 2000), pp. 104–7.
5. Debra E. Soled (ed), *China: A Nation in Transition* (Washington, D.C.: Congressional Quarterly Inc., 1995), pp. 55–6.
6. *Encyclopedia of Chinese Films*, 1949.10–1976, Vol. 3, p. 8.
7. Yao, *Qin Yi*, p. 267.
8. Qin Yi, *I Play All the Roles*.
9. Yao, op. cit., p. 270.
10. Ibid., pp. 272–8.
11. Qin Yi, op. cit.
12. Yao, op. cit., pp. 278–82.
13. Soled, op. cit., p. 56.
14. Clark, op. cit., pp. 36–1.
15. Lloyd E. Eastman, *The Abortive Revolution: China under Nationalist Rule, 1927–1937*, third printing (Cambridge, MA: Harvard University Press, 1990), pp. 311–2.
16. Interview, Qin Yi, December 15, 2005.
17. *Encyclopedia of Chinese Films*, Vol. 3, p. 65.
18. Cho, *Blooming Flower in Shanghai.*, p. 120.
19. *Encyclopedia of Chinese Films*, Vol. 3, p. 103.
20. Clark, op. cit., pp. 76–8.
21. Leyda, *Dianying, Electric Shadows*, p. 409.
22. Clark, op. cit., p. 106.
23. *Encyclopedia of Chinese Films*, Vol. 3, pp. 116–7.
24. Qin Yi, op. cit.
25. Soled, op. cit., pp. 59–62.
26. Rayns and Meek, *Electric Shadows*, pp. A6–A7.

27. Soled, op. cit., pp. 63–4.
28. *Encyclopedia of Chinese Films*, Vol. 3, p. 162.
29. Ibid., p. 146.
30. Yao, op. cit., pp. 287–99.
31. Interview, Jin Fei Heng, December 17, 2005.
32. Qin Yi, op. cit.
33. Interview, Jin Fei Heng, op. cit.
34. Qin Yi, op. cit.
35. Paul Clark, *Reinventing China: A Generation and Its Films* (Hong Kong: The Chinese University of Hong Kong, 2005), pp. 18–9.
36. Soled, op. cit., p. 64.
37. Xia Yan, "Remember the Past as a Lesson for the Future," trans. Fong Kenk Ho, *Dianying Yishu*, No. 1, 1979, in Rayns and Meek (eds), op. cit., pp. T10–T13.
38. Jonathan D. Spence, *The Gate of Heavenly Peace* (New York: Viking Press, 1981), pp. 341–7.
39. Clark, op. cit., pp. 94–5.
40. Paul G. Pickowicz and Yu Nien-Ch'ao, "Political and Ideological Themes in Chinese Films of the Early Sixties: A Review Essay," paper presented to the workshop on Contemporary Chinese Literature and the Performing Arts, John King Fairbank Center for East Asian Research, Harvard University, 1979.
41. R.R.C. de Crespigny, *China This Century*, p. 223.
42. Clark, *Reinventing China*, pp. 110–8.
43. Yao, op. cit., pp. 283–6.
44. Interview, Jin Fei Heng, op. cit.
45. Spence, op. cit., pp. 341–7.
46. Clark, op. cit., pp. 18–9.
47. R.R.C. de Crespigny, op. cit., pp. 245–6.
48. Paul J. Bailey, *China in the Twentieth Century* (Oxford, UK and Malden, MA: Blackwell Publishers, Ltd., 2001), pp. 180–2.
49. Rayns and Meek, op. cit., pp. B13–B14.
50. Ibid.
51. Ibid., p. A7.
52. Clark, op. cit., pp. 129–33.
53. Ibid., pp. 139–41.
54. Interview, Qin Yi, op. cit.

55. Clark, op. cit., p. 125.
56. Yomi Braester, *Witness against History: Literature, Film, and Public Discourse in Twentieth-Century China* (Stanford: Stanford University Press, 2003), pp. 109–11.
57. Ibid., pp. 111–5.
58. Leyda, op. cit., p. 285.
59. Braester, op. cit., p. 24.
60. Interview, Jin Fei Heng, op. cit.
61. Yao, op. cit., pp. 289–301.
62. Interview, Qin Yi, op. cit.
63. Robert Dallek, *Nixon and Kissinger: Partners in Power* (New York: HarperCollins Publisher, 2007), pp. 362–7.
64. Edwin E. Moise, *Modern China: A History* (London and New York: Longman, 1986), pp. 210–6.
65. Braester, op. cit., p. 131.
66. Moise, op. cit., pp. 216–7.
67. Michael Gasster, *China's Struggle to Modernize*, Second Edition (New York: McGraw-Hill, 1983), p. 160.
68. Braester, op. cit., p. 133.
69. Clark, op. cit., p. 160.
70. Paul Clark, "Chinese Cinema in the Second Half of the Seventies," paper presented to the Workshop on Contemporary Chinese Literature and the Performing Arts, Harvard University, June 1979, p. 15.
71. Soled, op. cit., p. 94.
72. Rayns and Meek (eds), op. cit., p. A12.
73. Yao, op. cit., pp. 340–2.
74. Qin Yi, op. cit.

CHAPTER 8

The Legacy of Jin Yan

I n death, Jin Yan suddenly took on a new importance. Leading individuals from the Ministry of Culture attended his funeral. Jin's wife, Qin Yi, his beloved step-daughter Jin Fei Heng, and a handful of film people were there. His son, Jin Jie, was too frightened to attend because his father had not yet been cremated and the son could not bear to view the corpse. The boy was present later when the actor's ashes were interred.

Jin Fei Heng recalled that when her father died and she saw his body "the sky had fallen."[1] The actor's mentor from the Golden Era of Shanghai, Sun Yu, attended but Wu Yonggang, his old friend, had died a few months earlier.

Huang Zongying, an actress, read the following eulogy at the brief ceremony:

> Turning into flame in the clouds, and leaving gold in the movie industry, Jin Yan did not shoot movies for fun or money. He wanted to leave something valuable for the generations to come.[2] [The Chinese characters for the name Jin Yan mean "gold" and "flame" respectively.]

After the funeral, Qin returned to the apartment and went onto the balcony and observed a solitary white blossom, the only remaining flower that Jin had planted. Day after day she watered it, hoping it would live. In her autobiography, the actress wrote:

> I don't know how much longer I will be able to see this little white flower, I think it must be like people and will eventually wither away. But I hope that the little white flower will continue to hold up its head ... Suddenly, there was a clear morning, when I pushed open the balcony door, twenty-four little white flowers were laughingly waving at me. "Ah, little flower, little flower, you're so good, you've never disappointed me, you also make me summon up courage to live!" I wanted to tell everything in my heart to the little white flowers. But the little white flowers, after they had bloomed so gloriously this time, gradually dried up. After this, they never sprouted again. All of them had withered. In the end, they had followed their master who had cultivated them in the first place, never to come back.[3]

Qin Yi never remarried. She continued to take care of Jin Jie and arranged for him to study painting. The actress took up the cause of the handicapped in China and appeared in the first film to treat the subject with dignity and understanding. She continued to make films and became a director of Shanghai TV Corporation. Her son's paintings started to sell. Actor Arnold Schwarzenegger, visiting the city, purchased one of Jin Jie's works for $25,000.[4]

The Cultural Revolution had been the most difficult period in the life of Jin Yan and Qin Yi, as it was for millions of Chinese. Their four-year separation from one another is best illustrated by the poet Chen Ming who was married to famous writer Ding Ling. He wrote:

> Dark nights pass and dawn comes.
> Bitter-cold days will turn to spring breezes.

If wild winds and rain didn't beat down on soft shoots,
How would mighty trees ever grow?[5]

Although Jin and Qin had marital problems prior to the Cultural Revolution, that event sealed any possibility that they could ever return to their earlier relationship. Coupled with that situation, Jin's worsening illness made it imperative for him to keep sleeping in a separate room. Yet, Qin remained loyal to him until his death. She blamed herself for his demise due to her busy schedule shooting movies but it was evident that his years of drinking and smoking as well as the disastrous stomach removal were the causes. The actor's sudden fall from fame too must have contributed to his poor health.

When one examines Jin's career and his accomplishments, it is clear his life was important to the growth of the Chinese film industry. One of the most popular stars of the 1930s, he was nicknamed the "Chinese Valentino."[6] After moving to Shanghai in 1927, within a few years, he was Lianhua's top male performer. He starred in the major productions of that studio and was voted "The Emperor of Film" in a newspaper poll.

Jin was not afraid to associate with leftist filmmakers and participate in their progressive productions. He was on the KMT blacklist, but was never arrested due to his popularity. The actor was fortunate to have several mentors such as Sun Yu, Tian Han, and others during his early days in Shanghai. He returned their gifts by assisting many young actors in their careers. He also was responsible for influencing Ruan Ling-yu in becoming anti-imperialist and making films which were veiled criticisms of the KMT regime and the status quo.

Jin's professional life was truly that of a perfectionist and hard worker. His acting style was one of naturalism and he refused to take parts in films in which he was asked to be phony. Often he would speak to a director and persuade him to change the interpretation of the character he played. The actor had appeared on the stage and had studied Shaw, Gorky, and other playwrights whose plays required a new type of acting. The old, flamboyant, declamatory style of performing was replaced by this new method of naturalism. Stress was placed on the "real-life" aspects — the inner, not the outer man.[7]

Actor Hardie Albright describes the style adopted by Jin Yan:

> Freudian theories were translated into acting terms. What appeared on the surface was only a part, or perhaps none, of the "real" meaning hidden underneath. No longer could an actor pick up a manuscript and interpret a character. It required time to get inside such characters. It was not wise to make snap judgments or depend upon tested and reliable devices of voice, gesture, or timing. The *need* had arrived for a new acting style.[8]

Jin's natural performances may have been a reason that censors overlooked some of his roles. It might explain why he often was seen on the screen bare-chested. In addition, this method according to Albright, "… could be understood by the butcher and baker."[9]

The Japanese occupation of Shanghai forced Jin to leave for wartime capital Chongqing with his first wife Wang Renmei. There were few opportunities to make many films, but the actor appeared in plays performed for the Chinese troops. When the hostilities ended, he returned to Shanghai after having divorced Wang. There he encountered actress Qin Yi whom he married in 1947. They both made several films before the victory of the CCP over the KMT in 1949 and the establishment of the PRC. Qin's career continued to progress, while Jin's tapered off. He was chosen to be head of the Actor's Guild, while his wife received important roles on the screen. Qin became a member of the CCP, but Jin never joined. He supported their movement and worked hard for the New China, but for a variety of reasons chose not to link up with the party.

After the Cultural Revolution, Jin continued to deteriorate, while Qin still pursued her screen career. His death was hardly noticed except by his family and friends. At the time of the 100th anniversary of Chinese cinema in 2005, his life was rediscovered by a new generation of filmgoers. Jin's photo and story are prominently displayed at the beautiful new National Film Museum in Beijing. VCDs and DVDs of his films are being released and Chinese television has telecast some of his early productions.

The public today can discover Jin Yan's many screen roles. They include brilliant performances as a coolie, farmer, movie star, bandit, revolutionary, sailor, soldier, Tibetan, Imperial official, student, landlord, musician, playboy, cadre, writer, worker, miner, blacksmith, cadet, and film extra. His life spanned the most turbulent period in modern Chinese history. He never forgot his Korean roots and fought against Japanese aggression through his films. Qin Yi's final thoughts about her husband are: "He was a man's man, but he had his soft side."[10] His epitaph at the Fu Shou Yuan Memorial Hall where his ashes are kept reads: "He was the most powerful actor who had the biggest influence on the progressive film industry."[11]

After being erased from the memory of the Chinese people for two generations, Jin Yan has re-emerged. Thanks to the Beijing Film Museum and television presentations of his films, the former "Emperor of Film" is being resurrected. The link between his style and that of other film icons is more readily apparent. For example, the current development of cinema in China is strikingly similar to the commercial model of movie-making in 1930s Shanghai. Jin, therefore, as the star leading man at that time can be compared with the present-day Jackie Chan. Both actors did their own stunts and displayed enormous physicality. The two stars also shared the love of women and fan adulation. They developed their roles into ones reflecting progressive politics and supreme athleticism. Jackie Chan made it to Hollywood, but Jin Yan decided not to go. Instead, he remained and contributed to the New China, only to be forgotten until now.

Notes

1. Interview, Jin Fei Heng, op. cit.
2. Wang Renmei, *Wo de cheng ming yu bu xing*, p. 195.
3. Qin Yi, op. cit., pp. 252–3.
4. Interview, Qin Yi, op. cit.
5. Spence, *The Gate of Heavenly Peace*, op. cit., pp. 349–50.
6. Yingjin Zhang and Zhiwei Xiao, *Encyclopedia of Chinese Films* (London and New York: Routledge, 1998), p. 204.
7. Hardie Albright, *Acting: The Creative Process*, Second Edition (Encino and Belmont, California: Dickenson Publishing Company, Inc., 1974), pp. 248–9.
8. Ibid., p. 249.
9. Ibid., p. 248.
10. Interview, Qin Yi, op. cit.
11. Cho Pock-rey, "The Emperor of Shanghai Movies," p. 211.

Interview with Qin Yi, Shanghai, PRC — December 15, 16, 17, 2005

Richard J. Meyer: Where did you see films in the 1930s?

Qin Yi: Shanghai.

RJM: Do you remember what theater and what year?

QY: The cinema downstairs from my office was built in the 1920s and I saw some of them there.

RJM: Do you remember how old you were when you saw your first film?

QY: I was seven when I started to see movies. Most of the films I saw were ones with Ruan Ling-yu. I particularly remember *The Peach Girl.*

RJM: Were you in Shanghai during the Japanese occupation or did you and your family go to Chongqing?

QY: Before the Japanese got to Shanghai I left by myself. The routes across the country were cut off and I went first to Hong Kong.

RJM: You traveled from Shanghai to Hong Kong?

QY: Yes, I took a boat. From Hong Kong, I took the train. It was called the Vietnamese/Chinese railroad. At that time, the front line was in Chongqing. Not everyone in the city was fighting the Japanese but there were a few people. I was involved and joined the Red Cross.

RJM: How old were you?

QY: Fifteen. I was in high school.

RJM: You left high school to join the troops?

QY: The Red Cross unit was actually in the school. I didn't leave school. I went as a high school student to the front line.

RJM: Did you go with your class?

QY: There were five girls who were in the Red Cross in my high school. Three of them were sacrificed in the war. I was just a freshman.

RJM: You were an early patriot!

QY: I didn't understand very much. I hated the fact that the Japanese had invaded. There were a lot of refugees from the northeast, which they lost. They came down and they would sing songs about refugees and that kind of music had a big influence on me.

RJM: What about your parents; your mother and father?

QY: I came from a big feudal family and its members all took the imperial civil service examination.

RJM: Were they from Shanghai?

QY: Yes, although they were originally from Pudong.

RJM: What happened during the Japanese invasion?

QY: Originally, we had a big family. When the occupation occurred, they all split up and they moved into the international section for safety — the former government was powerless. It was like every country in the world had a concession in Shanghai. They had a French concession, they had an English concession, and they had all sorts of international concessions. At that time, people called Shanghai "the adventurer's paradise." The Chinese had very few areas for themselves.

RJM: In 1941, the Japanese took over the concessions. What happened to your parents then?

QY: My parents stayed in Shanghai with my brothers and sisters. My family members did ordinary jobs like teaching and things like that.

RJM: After you went to Chongqing, what else did you do?

QY: I was in Chongqing for seven years and Chengdu for one year. At that time, it was relatively open because the Japanese army couldn't go in; they just bombed.

RJM: I've seen the caves and tunnels in Chongqing. It must have been very dangerous with the bombing.

QY: Yes, it was very dangerous. The caves were not very sturdy. One time a bomb fell and the front of the cave collapsed — 20,000 people were killed inside. When I heard the alarm, I would run into the air raid shelter and when I came out my home was gone. It was easier to be by myself during the air raids. I was so young at that time. I was so against the bombing and there was so much hatred of the Japanese invasion. Their kind of invasion was very savage. I heard it with my own ears and experienced it myself. I saw the actual results of the Japanese aggression. My other family members stayed in Shanghai because they were doing regular jobs. Everyday my sister would have to pass over a certain bridge; the Japanese would be on the bridge occupying it and they would always find ways to humiliate her. They had attack dogs that would come and attack her. If it didn't bite her, it would jump on her back and knock her down on the ground. She would try to run away. She said that this kind of humiliation was worse than killing you.

RJM: I read about that. It was terrible. Getting back to your experience in Chongqing, what were you doing there? Were you still with the Red Cross? How did you get involved with the film industry?

QY: It was a very mysterious circumstance. At that time, when I was leaving for the front line, I actually wanted to go to Yan'an but all of the roads were cut off. There was only one road open and that was to Chongqing. I went with a schoolmate. My opposition to the Japanese was very strong. I didn't know very much about what was going on. I stayed in the YWCA. It was run by a church group. I only had $20 and to stay at the YWCA, including room and board, it was $16 per month. I paid $16 and I knew I could stay for at least one month. When you are at a young age, you don't know about fear. According to the Chinese calculation, I was only seventeen, which would be sixteen in the United States. I went with some of my YWCA friends to see a play. I went into the play and the person who brought me went to the restroom. I didn't know that it was one of the directors but one of the directors came walking around, saw me and stopped. He said, "Hey little girl, where are you staying?" I told him that I was nowhere and had just arrived a few days ago. He asked me if I liked to act and I told him I had never done it before. He asked me if I was interested in it and I told him no. He told me, "If you like to watch plays as you do tonight then see them as much as you would like and if you are ever interested come visit me." He asked me where I lived and I told him the YWCA. He had given me something to fill out, if I was interested. They called me and changed my name. Originally it was three characters: Qin Dehe. "If you want to act, you can come tomorrow or the next day." This is how I started and just blindly got into it.

RJM: You like acting?

QY: I liked to watch but because I came from a feudal family, I was very shy and reserved. I felt it was embarrassing.

RJM: But you did it anyway.

QY: I needed the money to live. After only one month they told me to go up on stage. Acting in a play is actually much harder than being in a movie because in a movie you do it line by line, but in the play I had to pay attention to everything: my hands, how I walked, etc. Later, when I was shooting movies, it was line by line or scene by scene. The director really helped me a lot.

RJM: Did that ultimately lead to your first film?

QY: At that time, in Chongqing, I shot four films. The plots were all very simple. They were all about fighting the Japanese. The characters were not very complicated. I felt it was easy and could force myself to do it. It was basically a story about the imperialists coming and fighting back. I also had personal feelings in the roles.

RJM: When did you start acting in films?

QY: At the end of 1938 I took part in the Chinese film industry. In 1941 I went into an acting troupe. It was all on the stage.

RJM: Did it tour?

QY: That was another group. The second group that I joined was secretly led by the Communists.

RJM: This is how you got involved with the Revolution?

QY: Yes.

RJM: Didn't they have to be undercover because the KMT controlled Chongqing?

QY: It was very easy for me to be in the second group. The reason why I got there was because one of the two directors that first spotted me actually took me over to the other group. Even though I couldn't do any acting, he saw me and thought I could be an actor. He is a very experienced director. His name is Ying Yunwei. When I was in the Chinese Film Company he was working there as well. After 1941, in Chongqing, I always did stage productions.

RJM: When did you meet your so-called first husband?

QY: I met my first husband when I was in the Chinese Film Company. At that time, he was a leading man. He was also a very good actor with a lot of experience. He was older than I by eleven years.

RJM: He was the one who introduced you to Jin Yan and Wang Renmei?

QY: Yes. He took me to meet them. The first time I met Jin Yan was also in Chongqing.

RJM: Did you talk to him the first time you met?

QY: No. He didn't say anything. He basically wouldn't talk to anybody. I was really disappointed because I was a fan of his. When he came there I was really excited and wanted to meet him. He wouldn't speak to anybody so people called him the "Emperor of Film." I was disappointed to find that the Emperor of Film was so arrogant. I wasn't arrogant myself but I saw that he was so arrogant so I decided to not pay any attention to him. I didn't take any initiative speaking to him.

RJM: Do you think during his early career, when he was so famous in Shanghai, that the fame went to his head a little?

QY: Later when I met him, I found he was not like that. He wasn't that arrogant. He didn't like to talk casually. He liked to do practical things.

RJM: He didn't like small talk?

QY: Yes. That is right. I saw the marriage between Jin Yan and Wang Renmei as extremely ideal because she was very outgoing. She had a lot of energy. At that time, I wasn't having very much contact with her husband. I sometimes asked myself what if Jin Yan and Wang Renmei had stayed together. This kind of tragedy can't be separated from the turbulent times that we were having.

RJM: What finally happened to Wang Renmei?

QY: She died in a really bad way. She married a painter named Ye Qianyu. He was actually still in love with his earlier wife, who was a dancer, so he wasn't very good to her. The former wife of the painter is still alive. She is in her nineties. She is English.

RJM: Was Wang Renmei young when she died?

QY: She was almost eighty. When she was dying, her husband didn't go to see her. After she was divorced from Jin Yan, she regretted it and always wanted to be married again.

RJM: Were you friendly with her?

QY: I knew her and was her fan. I hoped the two of them wouldn't get divorced.

RJM: Later on, when you became famous, did you see her occasionally?

QY: I was in a film called *Two Family Village*. At that time, I was rising and she was going down. I played the leading role as a farm girl and Wang Renmei had a supporting role.

RJM: You two were friendly even though she had been married to Jin Yan?

QY: I felt sorry for her. We were friendly.

RJM: Did she ever tell you why the first marriage broke up?

QY: She never said.

RJM: Do you have a feeling?

QY: I felt Wang Renmei regretted getting divorced. But she knew Jin Yan had already remarried so there was nothing she could do.

RJM: Do you have any idea why Wang Renmei and Jin Yan ended their marriage?

QY: They were in Shanghai and the Japanese wanted him to shoot movies for them but he refused. They sent military police to arrest him. He and Wang Renmei escaped. It was a very difficult time. At that time, the U.S. military was there. Her English was good and she was a good typist. She wanted to go work for the Americans as a typist and he absolutely refused.

RJM: Getting back to the disagreement between Jin Yan and Wang Renmei — she wanted to work for the Americans and he didn't want that?

QY: He said absolutely not.

RJM: What was his reason?

QY: It was because Jin Yan was very reserved. He didn't have many friends. Only a few directors like Wu Yonggong. She was so outgoing, extroverted, and this was why.

RJM: Do you think also that he didn't like the fact that the Americans were supporting the KMT and not the CCP?

QY: Yes.

RJM: I just had a feeling that this was one of the reasons. Did she work for the Americans?

QY: She went to work for them. Jin Yan opposed strongly and then she had to quit her job. They would have emotional breaks that added up. There were a lot of arguments. After they divorced, they were still good friends. In the past, they had gone hunting together and things like that. Sometimes she and Jin Yan would talk about old times and I would go into another room.

RJM: Were you jealous?

QY: No. I wasn't jealous. I have a very delicate or soft heart. When they were starting to shoot films together, Wang Renmei was already starting to have some mental problems. For example, she was often saying to herself, "Jin Yan. Jin Yan." I was very sympathetic to her. I had empathy for her. After her illness worsened, she was sent to Beijing to a specialized hospital. I told Jin Yan that she was healthy and strong. I said, "If Wang Renmei gets better and you want to get back together with her or take care of her, that's fine."

RJM: What did he say?

QY: He got really mad. He said, "Where in the world would there ever be somebody like this?" He said, "If I ever wanted to get back together with her I never would have divorced nor would I have married you." He said, "Don't raise this issue again, it is too ridiculous."

RJM: It sounds like he was very dramatic!

QY: I am also dramatic.

RJM: Two dramatic people!

QY: When I think about a situation, I will think first about the other person.

RJM: If you don't mind talking about it, I am still interested in your first marriage only as it relates to you, as a person, and your children.

QY: The first marriage was unfortunate because I did not have any feelings for him. It wasn't that there was anything wrong with the marriage — he was an alcoholic. It affected his work, everything at home, etc. so it was impossible to live with him. I thought since I was married I would try to do all I could to save it but I couldn't do it.

RJM: Did you have children from that marriage?

QY: One daughter. She is now over sixty.

RJM: She is well?

QY: Yes. She is with me. I gave her up for two years and then fought to get her back.

RJM: When you were married to Jin Yan did your daughter live with you?

QY: Yes.

RJM: How did they get along?

QY: Good. She recognized him as a father.

RJM: And he recognized her as a daughter?

QY: She knew that she had a real father because she was only five when they brought her back.

RJM: He treated her as a real daughter and she treated him as a real father?

QY: Yes.

RJM: When you left the marriage, you had to take care of your daughter or did she live with relatives?

QY: At that time, my former husband had a girlfriend. It was 1945 when I brought my daughter back. My ex went with the girlfriend to some other place. After that, I came back to Shanghai.

RJM: You were living with your daughter in Shanghai when Jin Yan made the famous call to your home?

QY: When I went back to Shanghai I did not know Jin Yan, but it was there that he came to find me.

RJM: Your daughter was living with you then?

QY: Yes.

RJM: Do you have any idea why he went to find you in Shanghai? How many years had elapsed?

QY: At that time, Jin Yan had just come to Shanghai. He was staying in the house of another actor. This actor happened to be in a movie with me. The other actor said, "What should we do? There isn't anything else to do so let's go to Qin Yi's house."

It was the Spring Festival. When he came, he sat for a while in my house. The second time, he visited by himself. He spoke a lot of different languages. Not counting his own Korean, the languages of the northeast, Mandarin, and good Shanghainese. He could speak really good Shanghainese. In my family, everyone spoke a real Shanghai dialect. He could communicate with them very well.

RJM: When you went back to Shanghai in 1945, you got into the film business?

QY: Yes, my director was Wu Yonggong.

RJM: How did you like Wu?

QY: He had the same character as Jin Yan. He would show up at our house. He wouldn't say anything. He would fall asleep on the couch and then wake up and say, "I'm off!"

RJM: How was he as a director?

QY: He did all of the editing. However you acted was okay. In the end, it was all under his control.

RJM: When you finally got to Shanghai, after the war, how did you make your entry back into the film business? Did you know the people?

QY: When I was in Chongqing, I had already made it to the top ranks. There were four big women actors and I was one of them. When I arrived in Shanghai, Wu Yonggong heard about my arrival and he got in touch with me.

RJM: What was the studio's name?

QY: Lianhua. The film I was in was about when the Japanese come and try to bomb people. The story was about an air force pilot and I was the wife of the pilot. The pilot died and the only people that were left were the family members and me. The Japanese then tried to attack them and we fought back.

RJM: Did you work for Lianhua until liberation?

QY: I wasn't a part of the company, I was brought in special.

RJM: Did you make films for other companies?

QY: I was always employed as a freelance.

RJM: You were making films for different companies during this period?

QY: They were private companies. They also had a lot of Communist agents that were spread out within the different studios. At that time, I was not a member of the party. The Communists actually encouraged me to shoot films for a lot of different companies because that way I would have prestige and then I could speak on my own to different people about the various issues.

RJM: After liberation, did you continue to make films?

QY: Even before 1949, I had already taken part in a plan for the Shanghai Movie Company.

RJM: Which was the Communist Party film company?

QY: Yes. It was what the Communists supported.

RJM: You were one of the pioneers in planning the Shanghai film studios?

QY: Yes. Before it was established — even then I was involved. I participated with the CCP, in the organizational stages of the studio, and joined the Communist Party in 1956.

RJM: You must have been very happy during the liberation of Shanghai.

QY: I was. I marched for one day and one night.

RJM: It must have been a very joyous occasion.

QY: Very exciting.

RJM: Did you immediately start making movies once the Communists were controlling the city?

QY: Yes. During the 50s and 60s I was shooting all the way up until the Cultural Revolution.

RJM: I'd like to change the subject. When did you marry Jin Yan? I know you married him in Hong Kong.

QY: 1947.

RJM: What was he doing while you were planning for the eventual takeover of the city and the film industry?

QY: He was also involved with me.

RJM: He had the same revolutionary fervor as you?

QY: Yes. He had very strong fervor. All of the way into the beginning of the 30s, in the left-wing movement, he was involved.

RJM: I know that he influenced Ruan Ling-yu to become progressive. He gave her the script for *Three Women*, which was the first left-wing film to get through the censors.

QY: He had a lot of friends who went to Yan'an. He wanted to go to Yan'an but he had signed a contract with Lianhua for seven films and had only done five. In that kind of situation, if you leave, you have to pay the company back for the cost of the two other movies that you haven't done. When the Japanese occupied, he still had two movies that he hadn't made so he had to stay. The Japanese went to catch him so he had to leave.

RJM: I want to know about the romance before you married Jin Yan.

QY: Our romance was actually very simple and short. At that time, I was busy shooting a lot of films. Jin would go to our house. He didn't have anything to do so he would sit around the house with my family. My mother and sister would play mahjong. They said to him, "What can we do to entertain you?" He wanted to play with them. I never liked to play. My mother was a really good cook. Jin Yan was also a good cook. The two of them would also spend a lot of time talking about cooking. I would often sit there and listen to their discussion because I couldn't cook.

RJM: Your mother really liked him?

QY: Yes but he didn't talk to her very often about things relating to work.

RJM: Could you compare your acting style with Jin Yan's acting style?

QY: They are actually very similar. One difference is when I was younger I studied literature in school. He was totally self-taught. He went to the Nankai Middle School. When he went to high school, he studied architecture. I had a commonality with him which was that we both liked movies. One difference was that I wasn't actively seeking a job in movies but he was trying really hard to get into the movie business.

RJM: I was always impressed that both of you were supportive of the Revolution. Did you both join the Communist Party at the same time? Who went first and when was that?

QY: I joined in the 50s. He didn't join.

RJM: But, he was very high up in the leadership circles.

QY: He wasn't ethnic Korean in China, he was actually fully Korean.

RJM: If he was fully Korean then he couldn't join the Chinese Communist Party?

QY: The problem was there were those people from the 30s, who he was close to, who then became leaders. He didn't have a good feeling about them. In the 50s, he thought about joining but he wasn't that enthusiastic about joining. This is my guess — he was a perfectionist. Everything he wanted done in a perfect way. He may have felt that to be a Communist Party member he would have to do it perfectly. Maybe he felt he couldn't do it.

RJM: He wanted to be absolutely 100 percent with anything he did.

QY: That is right.

RJM: What did both of you do during the Cultural Revolution? From what I have heard from different people, it was a very difficult time period. What was your experience during that time?

QY: During the Cultural Revolution, everyone had difficulties. If you compare our difficulties to people who were really in bad straits, we were better off. I had a tougher time than he did. At that time, his illness was really bad and he basically went to the drama school and spent all of his time fixing all of the instruments and tools because that was something he could do.

RJM: Was that in Shanghai?

QY: Yes. I had a more difficult time because in the 50s, after liberation, I was really out in the limelight and made a lot of movies. I was also on a lot of committees and talked a lot. Later, they attacked four political cultural traitors — Zhou Yang, Qiam Han, Yang Han-shen, and Xia Niam; they were called "the four guys." They were leaders of political and cultural areas — one was the chief administrator of culture. I was considered to be their pet. They were the "four dudes or studs." They were attacked. The four were accused of being involved in dirty work. I had a difficult time. Jin Yan, during the 50s, made few movies so they couldn't pin anything on him. He hadn't done anything. He was staying at home doing his own stuff.

RJM: At that time, did you both live at home?

QY: He lived at home. I did not.

RJM: Where did you live?

QY: I and some others (for example, the deputy mayor and other officials) were all put in a correctional facility for young people in Shanghai.

RJM: Was it like a prison?

QY: It wasn't a prison — you had separate rooms but they would lock the door. It wasn't a prison but in a way it was like a prison. You had a room with one or two people.

RJM: Was the idea of why you were there to "reeducate" you?

QY: There were different reasons for putting people in there. One was to just keep an eye on the people. Another reason was to separate them or make people write confessions. The confessions were not about themselves, they were confessions about other people — to give information about other people. They wanted me to inform them about other people. I could not write, as I didn't know anybody. I had done a few movies but it was other people like the cultural minister that really knew a lot of people.

RJM: The fact that you weren't able to write, did they feel you were holding out or not cooperating?

QY: They also wanted me to write about my own past. For example, earlier I mentioned about when I was younger, in Chongqing, I went to the front with some troops. It turned out those were not Communist troops, they were KMT troops. I just wanted to get to the front. They didn't care that it was the front, they just said, "Oh, you were with the KMT." They wanted me to write about this.

RJM: Did you write about it?

QY: I wrote about it and wrote about how I had to take a test to get in, as a student. I also wrote the names of the others that also went in. I wrote what I did in the unit and how I came out. I only wrote once and I was in there for eight months total. I was in so long because they said I was a hardliner because I wasn't willing to write. I told them that I didn't have anything else to write. They told me that if I wrote more they would let me out early. They wanted me to write the story of my life from when I was first conscious all the way up until the Cultural Revolution. I asked them how I could remember what happened every day.

RJM: During those eight months were you in touch with Jin Yan?

QY: No, no contact whatsoever.

RJM: Did he tell you what he was doing during those eight months?

QY: You couldn't directly communicate with your family. You had to go through the people in charge. If I needed a pen or some clothing, I went through them and they would get in touch with my family. You couldn't directly speak to your family members, write letters, or anything.

RJM: But you could ask for pens, etc.? Did you get those?

QY: Yes. Originally it was eight months, but I was actually in there for two years. I wrote everything and because I couldn't write anymore, they went to get it from other sources and did their own research. They found out it was the same as what I had written. Of the three girls that were involved in the unit, they were checking on another girl and found out what I wrote and what she said was the same. When they found out it was the same they let me go.

RJM: Was it two years total in confinement or two years after the eight months?

QY: All together, two years.

RJM: Did you ask Jin Yan what it was like for the two years while you were away?

QY: He didn't say anything. He was at home all of the time. He went to the cadre school. When I got out, I went immediately to the cadre school because I knew that is where he was but they didn't let us meet.

RJM: When were you able to return?

QY: He came back to Shanghai first.

RJM: Where was the cadre school?

QY: It is near the ocean in Feng Xian County. We were with farmers who worked reclaiming land that had been salinated by the ocean. The farms there were where the educated youth in the cities were sent to.

RJM: When Jin Yan was at the school did he actually sleep there or did he have to sleep on the farm?

QY: All of us had to build our own houses. When I first arrived, we spent two to three days building our own houses and we slept in those.

RJM: Did you live there too?

QY: Yes. The men and women were separated. The women were on one side and the men were on the other.

RJM: Did you voluntarily go there to see Jin Yan and then you had to stay — is that what happened?

QY: I didn't know he was there. After I was released from the Shanghai facility, I was sent to the cadre school and from there we had to go to the countryside.

RJM: But you didn't know that Jin Yan was right next door in Feng Xian?

QY: Even if I made a request to see him it wouldn't have worked. I was sent there without knowing Jin was there.

RJM: When did you learn that Jin Yan was at the cadre school?

QY: After I got there some people told me that he was also there but we didn't have any meeting. They had a lot of very strange ways of doing things.

RJM: How long were you at the farm at the school?

QY: About two years. Jin Yan was only there for one year because he had health problems.

RJM: They let him go back to Shanghai?

QY: Yes.

RJM: While you were at the correctional institute for young people for two years, he was still in Shanghai and then he was sent to the cadre school for one year and released. You were there for another year, correct?

QY: For the two years that I was in the correctional facility he was in Shanghai but he was sent a little earlier. Then, he came back earlier and I stayed for another year.

RJM: When you finally returned to Shanghai, he was already there?

QY: After I was released, I came back to Shanghai but didn't do any shooting. They had me looking at scripts.

RJM: Did you go back to your apartment where Jin Yan was?

QY: I returned home and we lived together.

RJM: What was it like when you first returned home after being separated for four years?

QY: There was one big change when I went back — when I was in the correctional institute my mother died and they didn't tell me.

RJM: I know it is painful to talk about the Cultural Revolution — I am really interested in the initial meeting that you had with Jin Yan after four years.

QY: When I returned from the Cultural Revolution, we were distracted. We had different kinds of feelings.

RJM: I'd like to change the subject. What was it like living in Hong Kong after World War II?

QY: In 1947, there was a split between the Nationalists and the Communists — everyone knew that there was going to be a civil war sooner or later. I and my friends had dealings with the Communists. The Communists felt that the people in artistic circles could leave Shanghai and spread ideas and then come back after liberation — this was okay. Going to Hong Kong was a little unnerving and dangerous. At that time, a director in Hong Kong asked me to go there and shoot a film. At that time, Jin Yan didn't have any offers in Hong Kong but he was in love with me so he decided to go with me. When we went to Hong Kong, he made the proposal of living together. If we were going to live separately it would have been more expensive. By saying let's live together, he was also saving money. I was working everyday — working hard and the director said, "If you are living together, why don't you get married?" It was arranged by friends. They took care of everything. When it came time for the wedding I took three days off and got married. Then I became pregnant. I had some complications and got sick so I decided to go back to Shanghai to have the baby and take care of it. Jin Yan thought about it and decided to go back with me

RJM: During this time, where did your daughter [from the first marriage] stay?

QY: At my home, with my mother.

RJM: When you went back to Shanghai, you became a leading lady of film. As I understand it, Jin Yan only played roles as supporting actor.

QY: When we went back to Shanghai, Jin Yan became the head of the group or union of actors. He was in charge of administration and it took a lot of time. He took jobs as supporting actor so it wouldn't interfere with his duties. After the liberation, he didn't express his artistic talents. In years later, he led a more "Western" lifestyle. In that period he pursued a lot of things. For example, he could do all sorts of sports: basketball, soccer, everything. He led this kind of life but then there was an attack on him. They said he was leading a bourgeois lifestyle. At that time his mood was very bad. The first thing to know is that Jin Yan came over to China with his father when he was a really little child. His father was a real patriot. His family had a certain amount of prestige. From when he was young, Jin Yan could do everything and fix everything. Being in control was always part of his character. Later, in Shanghai, some people would criticize him for his past. He would react by staying at home. He was in a very depressed mood. At one time, I told him not to worry — he didn't have to go out and act. Because I loved him I did not want him to be criticized. He did not agree. He thought I was just like them. He thought I was ridiculous — this was when he was very depressed. He did shoot six films at this time, even though he wasn't the star. They were good movies. Now when people look back and evaluate his films from that time, they realize the good job that he did do. They were very outstanding.

RJM: As I understand and have studied other stars, many times they are not happy from being the leading actor and going to a supporting role. How did he really feel about his new role as a supporting actor?

QY: He didn't say it directly, he kept it inside — gradually he lost his interest in films and art. For example, when we were at home watching television, he didn't want to watch any movies. He only wanted to watch sports. In the afternoon, he would watch his sports. When we viewed a movie together, we both were very absorbed by it. At the end, I said, "That was such a good movie." He asked, "In what way was it good?" I couldn't think of anything so I commented, "It was so realistic." He said, "Let me tell you something — it is not realistic. The director and actors know what the audience wants to see. It is like a trick for the audience." I realized that he was actually still interested in the arts and film. He had a lot of difficulties in his heart and wasn't talking about them. He wasn't good at acting in a political way. For example, he didn't like to "kiss-up" to the director. In the 30s, a lot of people that he had been friends with became leaders. After the liberation, he wasn't very close to them. He didn't have amicable relationships.

RJM: Do you think that is because he was a very proud person and therefore didn't want to "make nice?"

QY: Yes, that is right. He felt like friends were friends and when you are working that is work. You don't want to be hanging on the coat-tails of these people.

RJM: Some of the actors would take people out for drinks and be very diplomatic and political?

QY: Yes. They would "kiss-up." He wouldn't do that. He thought that he hadn't really acted in many films. During the war against Japan, he was only in two. After liberation he worked on a few films. He was twelve years older than I was. He was forty when he was feeling a lack of hope. Then after liberation he was in an administrative position. He wasn't able to do a lot. By the time he was forty, which was the peak of his career; there weren't any films for him.

RJM: When he was making these films, was he on salary or did he get paid per picture?

QY: After liberation, all together there were six films. There were no contracts at that time so everyone received a salary.

RJM: He was paid by the film studio or state?

QY: It was a state-run enterprise so it was the government.

RJM: He was paid whether he made a film or not?

QY: Yes. He received the highest pay. He was first class.

RJM: Part of his duties, in addition to making films, was the head of the actor's union?

QY: He was the head of the actor's organization. There were approximately 170 actors and he was the chief.

RJM: Was he appointed or elected by the actors?

QY: The government appointed him.

RJM: How long was he the head of that organization?

QY: He did this until 1960 when he had a stomach operation and then many after effects of the operation.

RJM: He must have been very effective as the head of the actor's organization.

QY: He was very good with the actors themselves. He got along well with them. He had a stubborn opinion. Sometimes when he was on the set with directors he would argue and get into quarrels with the directors. When he was in this position, sometimes the leaders would say something and he wouldn't pay attention to them. There were a lot of people he was close to during the 30s. After liberation, they went on and became leaders. After this, he did not see them in the same way. He didn't like them anymore.

RJM: Do you think it was because they felt powerful?

QY: They would criticize his way of life. He thought their criticism was wrong.

RJM: Do you think they criticized him because it was in fashion to criticize?

QY: There were a lot of people, after liberation, who had "defects." These people were being criticized. They didn't criticize Jin Yan only. He stuck out more than others. At that time, things were more immature. If he had lived until this moment, he wouldn't have any problems.

RJM: After Jin's long illness when did he die?

QY: He died on December 27, 1983. He was set aside for half a month; then the funeral; and after he was cremated. With the ashes, they did another ceremony. At first the box of ashes was not displayed. They were enclosed and put in a drawer and closed. You couldn't see the box, take pictures in front of it, or put flowers there. We moved it to a place in the suburbs of Shanghai, it is called Fushou Yuan. It is a memorial hall where they put ashes.

RJM: Was your son well enough to go to the funeral?

QY: I told him to go to the cremation and he said, "I'm afraid, please forgive me." When they were putting the ashes in place, he wanted to go to that. He didn't dare to see his dead father.

RJM: Was the body on display?

QY: His body was there on display before it was cremated (at the funeral home) and he didn't want to go view the body. In the ceremony with the ashes there was a box and my son kept his head down. My daughter went to all of the ceremonies.

RJM: When Jin Yan made films in the 30s, was he considered the symbol of the ideal Chinese male?

QY: The audience felt that way. He was the ideal. He had a great appearance. He was very pretty. He had a great body. Very few people, at that time, had a body like him. He was also very multi-talented.

RJM: Did he have many women throwing themselves at him?

QY: A lot of girls were pursuing him. After he died there was even a woman that wrote a letter. She wrote she had always pursued him but was never able to get him. She wrote it to Jin Yan. All of the attention caused a lot of hassle for him. Many were pursuing Jin Yan and interested in him. Sometimes he wasn't able to resist. He was this way to one young woman and it caused me a lot of pain. He told me that the person was ridiculous. There were also a lot of people within our circle that also pursued him. If he didn't pay attention to someone or ignored them it would cause the opposite effect. The person would get angry and say bad things. He was in a tough spot.

RJM: After he passed away, was there anything you found out that you didn't know before?

QY: I knew pretty much everything.

RJM: If you had to sum up your relationship with Jin Yan, how would you describe it?

QY: Jin Yan was very lucky to be born with very good traits. Sometimes those traits caused a lot of problems. If he ever said something bad, people would hate him. It took him a long time to love someone, as in the case with me.

RJM: During the 30s rumors were played up in the press. I am assuming that he was also a target of these lies.

QY: There was no way to put any limits on those newspapers. Now you can sue them.

RJM: Did he ever talk about people saying bad things about him?

QY: There was one time I remembered from the 1940s — it was before he became sick. He had a friend, Liu Qiong, and they went to a bar to eat. They brought two girls with them that were their friends. They weren't girlfriends that they wanted to marry. A guy in the bar was jealous and said something. Jin Yan was a good boxer and fighter. He went over to the guy and knocked him out. It turned into a big bar fight. They pulled everyone back. Then, I read about it in the newspaper. I saw it in the big headline. He said it was nothing and the girls were just people that they were introduced to. It was also not beneficial to him. When there were people pursuing him he would sometimes have a change in thoughts. He would be shaken and unresolved in his thoughts.

RJM: Were you jealous when you read about him going to the bar with the girls?

QY: I was worried about him. I thought if the newspapers were writing this type of news it would not be good for him. I knew he wouldn't have any "real" type of thing going on.

RJM: You trusted him and knew that the newspaper was playing up the sensational aspect.

QY: The paper sold a lot of copies.

RJM: I have the impression that you were and are an extremely loyal person.

QY: When I married him, I wanted to grow old together. Sometimes, in reality, I wasn't able to achieve my desire. Jin Yan was so healthy and in such good shape. Then he was sick for over twenty years. I am very good with dealing with my own feelings. Things like this will happen to people. I had an awareness that anything could happen at any time. I felt if I could study more things and gain more knowledge it would be better in the long run. In the past, there were a lot of people pursuing me as well. I didn't pay attention to any of them. I only loved Jin Yan. However, this caused me to insult a lot of people and then they would say bad things about me. For example, there was a rumor that I had a child with a Soviet actor. I wondered how this would be possible!

RJM: Lu Xun said, "Gossip is a dangerous thing." You didn't let the gossip bother you?

QY: No. I just laughed.

RJM: Did it bother Jin Yan?

QY: No. He wouldn't believe it either.

RJM: Both of you laughed at the gossip.

QY: There were sometimes major effects from the gossip. Originally, they were going to make a joint Chinese and Soviet film. The director wanted me to play the part of the woman. Because of all the gossip of my having a child with a Soviet actor they decided not to.

RJM: So because of gossip you lost an opportunity.

QY: Even if you don't pay attention to rumors, they will sometimes have an effect. With Jan Yan there was more gossip. The gossip did have a big effect in the case of Jin Yan. After liberation, when he was working, he was getting the highest pay possible. I had heard that his pay was only two ranks less than Chairman Mao. People were very jealous. They would take the rumors and use them to attack him. He is still not recognized as the number one actor.

RJM: He should be on the same level as Ruan Ling-yu?

QY: She had more publicity because she committed suicide.

RJM: I hope my book will do something to elevate him to the highest ranks of Chinese actors.

QY: Theoretically, during the Cultural Revolution, he should have been severely attacked and possibly killed. Because there was a connection to the four studs — when they tried to review his movies and the way he shot them they were all excellent. They couldn't criticize him. They couldn't do anything. His weak point was that he liked to drink. Sometimes when he would get drunk he would forget what he had done. A lot of the occasions I didn't know about because he would go out with friends. When he was at home and got drunk he would do things like climbing up onto the roof and walking around in circles. It scared me. When I questioned him the next day he would deny it.

RJM: Do you think the drinking had something to do with his stomach problems?

QY: Yes. There was a connection. He was in a movie called *Eagles Brave the Storm*. In the film, they had to go up to the northwest. It was really cold and there was snow. They were living in a tent. They would have raw bear meat or other meat. They would cook it in the fire and heat it quickly. He also drank a lot of white wine. His stomach problems started during this time.

RJM: What did he drink?

QY: Chinese white liquor. He liked whiskey and brandy the most — imported.

RJM: They were all very high in alcohol.

QY: Yes. 50–60 percent. The Chinese white liquor was called white liquor or white wine (but it isn't really wine). Another thing he drank a lot of was beer. He drank sixteen bottles in one sitting.

RJM: Did you ever try to ask him not to drink so much?

QY: I would try to stop him but if I tried, he would drink even more.

RJM: You gave up?

QY: Yes. I didn't try to stop him. I let him drink.

RJM: Did the drinking interfere with his movie work?

QY: No. He wouldn't drink when he was working. He drank only when he wasn't working.

RJM: Was the drinking because he wasn't in the films?

QY: It is hard to say. Sometimes he would have problems in his heart so he would drink then. He also smoked a pipe. He did it all. He was coughing and coughing; he had cancer in his lungs and he would still smoke. He thought if he stopped smoking he would die right away.

RJM: If you had to use a phrase or sentence to describe Jin Yan, what phrase would you use?

QY: He was a man's man but he had his soft side.

RJM: Thank you very much for spending so much time with me.

QY: It was my pleasure.

Filmography of Jin Yan

Mu Lan Cong Jun (Hua Mulan Joins the Army)
1928, Minxin Motion Picture Company, black and white; Script and
    Director: Hou Yao; Camera: Liang Linguang; Actors: Jin Yan,
    Li Dandan, Liang Mengheng, Li Huamin, Xin Yi.

Re Xue Nan Er (Hot Blooded Man)
1929, Minxin Motion Picture Company, black and white; Director:
    Wan Laitian; Actors: Jin Yan, Wan Laitian, Yang Aili, Gao
    Zhanfei, Zuo Ming, Cai Chusheng.

Feng Liu Jian Ke (The Playboy Swordsman)
1929, Minxin Motion Picture Company, black and white; Script:
    Sun Yu; Director: Sun Yu; Actors: Jin Yan (Long Fei), Gao
    Qianping (Lu Xiaoxia), Gao Weilian (Bai Qi), Liu Jiqun (Niu
    Zhengfeng).

Yecao Xianhua (Wild Flower)
1930, Lianhua Studios, black and white; Director: Sun Yu; Music
    Composer: Sun Chengbi; Actors: Jin Yan, Ruan Ling-yu, Liu
    Jiqun.

Lian'ai Yu Yiwu (Love and Duty)

1931, Lianhua Studios, black and white; no sound; Director: Bu Wancang; Actors: Jin Yan, Ruan Ling-yu, Chen Yanyan, Liu Jiqun, Li Ying.

Yin Han Shuang Xing (Two Stars Shining in the Milky Way)

1931, Lianhua Studios, black and white; no sound; Director: Shi Dongshan; Actors: Jin Yan (Yang Yiyun), Zi Luolan (Li Yueying), Gao Zhanfei (Gao Qi), Ye Juanjuan, Chen Yanyan (actor), Song Weisai (Li Xudong), Liu Jiqun (assistant director), Wang Cilong, Zhou Wenzhu, Sun Yu, Tang Tianxiu, Cai Chusheng, Li Lili, Zhou Ke, Dong Shaofen.

Yi Jian Mei (A Spray of Plum Blossoms)

1931, Lianhua Studios, black and white; no sound; Director: Bu Wancang; Actors: Jin Yan, Ruan Ling-yu, Lin Chuchu, Chen Yanyan, Wang Guilin, Gao Zhanfei.

Taohua Qi Xue Ji (The Peach Girl)

1931, Lianhua Studios, black and white; no sound; Director: Bu Wancang; Actors: Jin Yan, Ruan Ling-yu, Wang Guilin, Zhou Lili.

Ye Meigui (Wild Rose)

1932, Lianhua Studios, black and white; no sound; Director: Sun Yu; Cast: Jin Yan (Jiang Bo), Wang Renmei (Xiao Feng), Ye Juanjuan (Su Qiu), Zheng Junli (Xiao Li), Wei Langen (Lao Qiang), Zhang Zhizhi (Xiao Feng Fu), Hong Jingling (Hu Jin), Liu Jiqun (Lao Niu).

Xu Gudu Chunmeng (Spring Dream in the Old Capitol II)
1932, Lianhua Studios, black and white; no sound; Director: Bu
   Wancang; Cast: Jin Yan (Huang Guoxiong), Ruan Ling-yu
   (Yanyan), Lin Chuchu (Wang Huilan), Zhou Boxun (Qu
   Huchen), Chen Yanyan (Zhu Ying).

San Ge Modeng Nuxing (Three Modern Women)
1932, Lianhua Studios, black and white; no sound; Director: Bu
   Wancang; Cast: Jin Yan (Zhang Yu), Ruan Ling-yu (Zhou
   Shuzhen), Li Zhuozhuo (Yu Yu), Chen Yanyan (Chen Ruoying),
   Han Langen (Zhu Ru), Wang Guilin (Zhang Yu's father), Chen
   Renzhi (Shu Zhen's mother) Gao Weilian (rich old man), Zhou
   Lili (female servant).

Ren Dao (Humanity)
1932, Lianhua Studios, black and white; no sound; Director: Bu
   Wancang; Cast: Jin Yan (Zhao Minjie), Lin Chuchu (Wu
   Ruolian), Li Zhuozhuo (Liu Xiyi), Wang Guilin (Zhao Shu),
   Li Jian (Ruolian's son), Li Ying (Liu Xiang), Jiang Junchao
   (LiWushi), Chen Yanyan (Miss Zhang).

Haiwai Juanhun (Cuckoo's Soul beyond the Seas)
1932, Lianhua Studios, black and white; no sound; Director: Jin
   Qingyu; Cast: Jin Yan (Zhong Zhigang), Zi Luolan (Yang
   Qihua), Yuan Congmei (Li Daosheng), Mrs. Chen (female
   servant), Chen Keke (the young Yang Qihua), Chen Shaohui
   (the young Zhong Zhigang).

Gong Yue Guo Nan (Going to Aid the Nation Together)
1932, Lianhua Studios, black and white; no sound; Directors: Cai
   Chusheng, Shi Dongshan, Sun Yu, Wang Cilong; Actors: Jin

Yan (volunteer soldier), Wang Cilong (Hua Weng), Gao Zhanfei (Changzi/eldest son), Song Wei (Ci Zi/second eldest), Deng Junli (San Zi/third son), Jiang Junchao (Si zi/fourth son), Zhou Wenshu (Chang Xi/eldest daughter in law), Ye Juanjuan (Ci Xi/second daughter in law), Chen Yanyan (Chang Nu/eldest daughter), Liu Jiqun (servant).

Chengshi Zhi Ye (City Nights)

1933, Lianhua Studios, black and white; no sound; Director: Fei Mu; Cast: Jin Yan, Li Junpan, Yang Tianxiu, Ruan Ling-yu, Li Keng, Wang Jialin, Zhou Lili, Wei Qianyuan, Ji Fansan, Zhang Meimei, Huang Junzhen, Liu Jiqun.

Mu Xing Zhi Guang (Maternal Radiance)

1933, Lianhua Studios, black and white; partial sound; Director: Bu Wancang; Actors: Jin Yan, Li Zhuozhou, Chen Yanyan, Lu Shi, He Feiguang, Li Junbi, Tan Ying, Liu Jiqun, Han Langen.

Da Lu (The Big Road)

1934, Lianhua Studios, black and white; sound; Director: Sun Yu; Cast: Jin Yan (Brother Gold), Zhang Yi (Zhang Yu), Deng Junli (Deng Jun), Luo Peng (Luo Ming), Zhang Zhizhi (Zhang Da), Chen Yanyan (Ding Xiang), Li Lili (Mo Li), Han Langen (the little sixth son of Han), Shang Guanwu (Hu Fu), Liu Liang (Liu Chang), Liu Jixu (old man Ding), Hong Jingling (Hong Jin).

Huang Jin Shidai (Golden Age)

1935, Yihua Enterprises, black and white; no sound; Director: Bu Wancang; Cast: Jin Yan (Chang Chun), Yin Mingzhu (Zhang Xiaomei), Hu Ping (Tao Li), Dai Yanfang (Li Yenong), Qing

Tong (Chang Chun Fu), Li Junpan (old professor), Zhang Zhizhi (Zhu Erhu), Qiu Yuanyuan (Ah Jin), Lei Linna (Ye Nongqi), Hu Jia (classmate), Qiang Yinqiu (classmate), Jin Yi (Ah Quan), Zhu Lang (Du Kun), Shen Zuoren (Li Zhengqing).

Xin Tao Hua Shan (New Peach Blossom Fan)
1935, Xinhua Enterprises, black and white; sound; Director: Ouyang Yuqing; Cast: Jin Yan (Fang Yumin), Hu Ping (Xie Sufang), Tong Yuejuan, Zhang Zhiyun, Wang Cilong, Dai Yanfang.

Zhuang Zhi Ling Yun (Soaring Aspirations)
1936, Xinhua Enterprises, black and white; sound; Director: Wu Yonggang; Cast: Jin Yan (Shun Er), Wang Renmei (Black Girl), Tian Fang (Tian Dehou), Zong You (Old Wang), Wang Cilong (Jian Xi), Han Langen (Monkey), Zhang Zhizhi (fatty), Chen Juanjuan (Black Girl as a child), Jin Lun (Shun Er as a child).

Dao Ziran Qu (Back to Nature)
1936, Lianhua Studios, black and white; sound; Director: Sun Yu; Cast: Jin Yan (Ma Long), Li Lili (Zhou Lihua), Bai Lu (Ah Mei), Zhang Zhizhi (General Zhou), Han Langen (Big Mr. Yang), Xu Jian (Zhou Meihua), Zong You (Niu Yuanzhang), Wu Jun (Mrs. Gu Lao), Ge Zuozhi (Shu Tong), Yin Xiuling (Chu Yi), Wen Rong (Ma fu), Xie Muli (Ah Lan).

Lang Tao Sha (Two Skeletons/Waves Washing the Sand)
1936, Lianhua Studios, black and white; sound; Director: Wu Yonggang; Cast: Jin Yan (Ah Long), Gong Zhihua (Ah Long's wife), Chen Juanjuan (young girl), Zhang Zhizhi (detective), Liu Liang (sailor), Shen Yuanming (captain).

Wu Song Yü Pan Jin Lian (Wu Song and Pan Jin Lian)

1938, Xinhua Enterprises, black and white; sound; Director: Wu
Tsai; Cast: Jin Yan (Wu Song), Gu Lanjun (Pan Jinlian), Xia
Lu (Wang Po), Liu Liang (Xi Menqing), Han Langen (Yun Ge),
Liu Jiqun (Wu Dalang), Hong Jingling (Zhang Dahu), Mei Xiu
(He Jiushu).

Qing Tian Xue Lei (Heaven Weeps Tears of Blood (Remake of *Love
and Duty*))

1938, Xinhua Enterprises, black and white; sound; Director: Bu
Wancang; Cast: Jin Yan (Li Zuyi), Yuan Meiyun (Yang Naifan),
Mei Xi, Gu Yelu, Zhang Zhizhi, Li Hong, Han Langen, Ye
Xiaozhu, Li Liying, Liu Jiqun, Hong Jingling, Bai She, Zhang
Fang.

Lin Chong Xue Ye Jian Chou Ji (Lin Chong, The Outlaw)

1938, Xinhua Enterprises, black and white; sound; Scriptwriter: Wu
Yonggang; Director: Wu Yonggang; Cast: Jin Yan, Li Hong,
Zhang Zhizhi, Sun Min, Hong Jingling.

Sai Shang Feng Yun (Storm on the Border)

1940, Xinhua Enterprises, black and white; sound; Director: Ying
Yunwei; Cast: Jin Yan, Li Lili, Shu Xiuwen, Zhou Feng, Wu
Yin, Chen Tianguo, Wang Ban, Zhang Jinde, Xu Shafeng, Han
Tao, Pan Zhiyan, Zhou Boxun, Jing Sen.

Chang Kong Wan Li (Wings of China)

1940, Central Movie Studios, black and white; sound; Director: Sun
Yu; Cast: Jin Yan, Bai Yang, Gao Zhanfei, Wang Renmei, Wei
Yiling, Gu Eryi, Shi Chao, Li Wei.

Shengli Jinxing Qu (Victory March)

1941, Xinhua Enterprises, black and white; sound; Director: Shi Dongshan; Cast: Jin Yan, the front line (soldiers) in Hubei and the local people.

Ying Chun Qu (A Spring Melody)

1947, Da Ye Film Studios, black and white; sound; Director: Wu Yonggang; Cast: Jin Yan (Dong Fangxi), Wang Di (Tiger 1), Zhang Zhizhi (Tiger 2), Liu Liang (Xiao Yiyun), Pei Chong (Li Wei), Hu Feng (temple sister), Fan Lai (A Fa), Liu Jie (A Fa's sister-in-law), Dai Qing (Big Hair), Liu Xiaojie (Second Hair), Tian Taixuan (old woman), Mo Qiu (Wife of Teacher Zhang), Chen Xiaowen (Yu Yu), Fang Bo (Bao Fahu), He Jianfei (owner of restaurant), Miao Zhusan (cattle herder), Dai Yanfang (Mr. Zhang), Tian Jun (doctor).

Sheng Long Kuai Xu (Riding the Dragon)

1948, Central Movie Enterprises Ltd., Second Studio, black and white; sound; Director: Yuan Jun; Cast: Jin Yan (Situ Yan), Li Pin (Mother Wang), Zhang Ying (Liu Nuoyan), Qin Xiaolong (Liu Xiaolong), Lin Zhen (Mrs. Hu), Lu Shan (Liu Wenlan), Bai Yang (Liu Wenhui), Zhou Wenbin (Cai Feng), Zhou Boxun (Master Han), Fei Bi (Mi Mi), Zhou Feng (Old Qiu), Mo Qiu (Miss Hu), Jin Gang (police chief), Miao Zhusan (Section Head Wang), Qiu Lu (Chief Editor Qiu), Fang Bo (Little Master Eight), Gu Chuhe (Little Xu) Dai Geng (Teacher Xiong), Lin Hua (sixth girl).

Shiqu de Aiqing (Lost Love)

1949, Guo Tai Studios, black and white; sound; Director: Tang Xiaodan; Cast: Jin Yan (Qin Fangqian), Qin Yi (Qiu Liyin).

Da Di Chong Guang (The Return of Spring)

1950, Shanghai Movie Making Factory, black and white; sound;
Script: Yuan Yunfan; Director: Xu Tao; Camera: Feng Sizhi,
Qiu Ge; Producer: Yue Lu; Actors: Jin Yan, Pan Wenzhan,
Zhang Zhen.

Wei Da De Qi Dian (The Great Beginning)

1954, Shanghai Movie Making Factory, black and white; sound;
Script: Ai Mingzhi; Director: Zhang Ke; Film: Huang Shaofen;
Co-director: Gao Heng; Cast: Jin Yan (Minister Nie), Zhang Fa
(Lu Zhongkui), Tang Huada (Chen Xiangqun), Chen Tianguo
(Li Yonghua), Gao Zheng (Lin Wenbing).

Mu Qin (Mother)

1956, Shanghai Movie Making Factory, black and white; sound;
Script: Hai Mo; Director: Ling Zifeng; Camera: Zhu Jing;
Producer: Jiang Yusheng; Actors: Jin Yan (Old Deng), Zhang
Ruifang (the mother), Zhang yi (Wang Laode), Zhang Ziliang
(Liang Chengwen).

Bao Feng Yu Zhong De Xiong Ying (Eagles Brave the Storm)

1957, Changchun Movie Making Factory, black and white; sound;
Script: Shi Lu; Director: Wang Yi; Film: Bao Jie; Producer:
Hao Weiguang; Cast: Jin Yan (Lao Ba'er), Sun Yu (Huo Wa),
Bai Dezhang (Military Commander Liu), Liang Yin (Zhang
Dashun), Song Baoyi (Zhou Heidan), Guo Zhenqing (Hua
Erdan), Lin Ruwei (Dan Guo).

Hai Shang Hong Qi (Red Flag over the Sea)

1958, Tian Ma Motion Picture Company, black and white; sound;
Script: Lu Junchao; Director: Chen Gang; Camera: Peng Enli;

Music Composer: Lu Qiming; Audio Recording: Huang Dongping; Producer: Mo Huiqian; Music: Shanghai Motion Picture Factory Orchestra; Actors: Jin Yan (Secretary Tang), Bai Mu (chief mate), Tie Niu (political commissioner of the party), Dong Lin (captain of the ship), Zhou Han (worker in charge of repair of the machine), Shi Jiufeng (helm worker), Xie Yibing (the old lady), Qiu Yuefeng (British captain).

Ai Chang Ru Jia (Love the Factory as Your Home)
1958, Jiangnan Motion Picture Factory, black and white; sound; Script: Zhao Ming; Director: Zhao Ming; Camera: Feng Sizhi; Actors: Jin Yan (district industry director), Zhang Ziliang (Liu Guorong, the factory head), Jiang Shan (Old Peng), Chen Zhijian (chairman of the worker's union), Yang Gongmin (A Xiang), Wu Qi (Xiao Tong), Yu Ding (Sheng Jiahai).

Sources for Jin Yan's Films

DVDs

San Francisco Silent Film Festival
833 Market Street
San Francisco, CA 94103
www.silentfilm.org

VCDs

www.hkflix.com
www.yesasia.com

35mm

China Film Archive
No. 3, Wen Hui Yuan Road, Xiao Xi Tian
Haidian District
100088 Beijing, China
Fax: 86-10-6225-9315
Email: cfafad@263.net

Chinese Taipei Film Archive
4F, No. 7 Ching-Tao East Road
Taipei 100, Taiwan
Fax: 886-2-2392-6359
Email: fact@m512.hinet.net
www.ctfa.org.tw

Bibliography

Books

1995 Pordenone Silent Film Festival Program. Gemona: Le Giornate del Cinema Muto, 1995.

1997 Pordenone Silent Film Festival Program. Gemona: Le Giornate del Cinema Muto, 1997.

Albright, Hardie. *Acting: The Creative Process*. Second edition. Encino and Belmont, California: Dickenson Publishing Co., Inc., 1974.

Andrew, Dudley J. *The Main Film Theories: An Introduction*. London, Oxford, New York: Oxford University Press, 1976.

Aumont, Jacques, Bergala, Alain, Michel, Marie, and Vermet, Marc. *Aesthetics of Film*. Translated and revised by Richard Newport. Austin: University of Texas Press, 1994.

Bailey, Paul J. *China in the Twentieth Century*. Oxford and New York: Basil Blackwell, 1988.

Bailey, Paul J. *China in the Twentieth Century*. Second edition. Oxford, UK and Malden, MA: Blackwell, 2001.

Barlow, Tani E. (ed). *Fortunes of Colonial Modernity in East Asia*. Durham and London: Duke University Press, 1997.

Berry, Chris. *Chinese Cinema*. Worcester: The Trinity Press, 1991.

Berry, Chris (ed). *Perspectives on Chinese Cinema*. London: British Film Institute, 1991.

Bisson, T.A. *Japan in China*. New York: Macmillan, 1938.

Boggs, Joseph M. and Petrie, Dennis W. *The Act of Watching Films*. Sixth edition. New York: McGraw Hill, 2004.

Braester, Yomi. *Witness against History: Literature, Film, and Public Discourse in Twentieth-Century China*. Stanford: Stanford University Press, 2003.

Brandy, Leo and Cohen, Marshall (eds). *Film Theory and Criticism: Introductory Readings*. Fifth edition. New York and Oxford: Oxford University Press, 1999.

Browne, Nick, Pickowicz, Paul G., Sobchak, Vivian, and Yau, Esther. *New Chinese Cinemas: Forms, Identities, Politics*. Cambridge: Cambridge University Press, 1994.

Cheng, Jim. *An Annotated Bibliography for Chinese Film Studies*. Hong Kong: Hong Kong University Press, 2004.

Cho, Pock-rey. *Blooming Flower in Shanghai: The Emperor of Shanghai Movies of the 1930s, Jin Yan*. Seoul: Juluesung Press, 2004.

Chow, Rey. *Primitive Passions: Visuality, Sexuality, Ethnography of Contemporary Chinese Cinema*. New York: Columbia University Press, 1995.

Chow, Tse-tsung. *The May Fourth Movement*. Cambridge, MA: Harvard University Press, 1960.

Clark, Paul. *Chinese Cinema: Culture and Politics since 1949*. Cambridge: Cambridge University Press, 1987.

Clark, Paul. *Reinventing China: A Generation and Its Films*. Hong Kong: The Chinese University Press, 2005.

Coble, Parks, M. Jr. *The Shanghai Capitalists and the Nationalist Movement, 1927–1937*. Second edition. Cambridge, MA and London, England: Council on East Asian Studies, Harvard University, 1986.

Dallek, Robert. *Nixon and Kissinger: Partners in Power*. New York: HarperCollins, 2007.

de Crespigny, R. R. C. *China This Century*. Sydney: Thomas Nelson, 1975.

Dissanayake, Wimal (ed). *Melodrama and Asian Cinema*. New York: Cambridge University Press, 1993.

Dong, Stella. *Shanghai: The Rise and Fall of a Decadent City*. New York: HarperCollins, 2000.

Dudden, Alexis. *Japan's Colonization of Korea: Discourse and Power*. Honolulu: University of Hawaii Press, 2005.

Eastman, Lloyd E. *Seeds of Destruction: Nationalist China in War and Revolution*. Stanford: Stanford University Press, 1984.

Eastman, Lloyd E. *The Abortive Revolution: China under Nationalist Rule, 1927–1937*. Third printing. Cambridge, MA: Harvard University Press, 1990.

Eastman, Lloyd E, Ch'en, Jerong, Pepper Suzanne, and Van Slyke, Lyman P., *The Nationalist Era in China: 1927–1949*. Cambridge: Cambridge University Press, 1991.

Ehrlich, Linda C. and Dosser, David. *Cinematic Landscapes: Observations on the Visual Arts and Cinema of China and Japan*. Austin: University of Texas Press, 1994.

Eisenstein, Sergei. *Film Forum: Essays in Film Theory*. Edited and translated by Jay Leyda. New York: Meridian Books, 1957.

Encyclopedia of Chinese Films. Volumes 1 (1905–1930, 2 (1931–1949), 3 (1949.10–1976). Beijing: China Movie Publishing House, 1996.

Fairbank, John King. *China: A New History*. Cambridge, MA and London: The Belknap Press of Harvard University Press, 1992.

Fu, Poshek. *Between Shanghai and Hong Kong: The Politics of Chinese Cinema*. Stanford: Stanford University Press, 2003.

Fu, Poshek. *Passivity, Resistance and Collaborators: Intellectual Choices in Occupied Shanghai, 1937–1945*. Austin: University of Texas Press, 1997.

Fu, Poshek and Desser, David (eds). *The Cinema of Hong Kong: History, Arts, Identity*. Cambridge: Cambridge University Press, 2000.

Gasster, Michael. *China's Struggle to Modernize*. New York: McGraw-Hill, 1983.

Gernet, Jacques. *A History of Chinese Civilization*. Cambridge, NY: Cambridge University Press, 1996.

Goto-Shibata, Harumi. *Japan and Britain in Shanghai, 1925–1931*. New York: St. Martin's Press, 1995.

Hauser, Ernest O. *Shanghai: City for Sale*. New York: Harcourt Brace, 1940.

Hu, Jubin. *Projecting a Nation: Chinese National Cinema before 1949*. Hong Kong: Hong Kong University Press, 2003.

Hutchings, Graham. *Modern China: A Guide to a Century of Change*. Cambridge, MA: Harvard University Press, 2001.

Johnstone, William Crane, Jr. *The Shanghai Problem*. Stanford, Stanford University Press, 1937.

Jones, Andrew F. *Yellow Music*. Durham and London: Duke University Press, 2001.

Kang, Man-Gil. *A History of Contemporary Korea*. Folkestone, UK: Global Oriental, 2005.

Kim, Djun Kil. *The History of Korea*. Westport, CN: Greenwood Press, 2005.

Knoshu, Harry H. *Celluloid China: Cinematic Encounters with Culture and Society*. Carbondale: Southern Illinois University Press, 2002.

Kracauer, Siegfried. *Theory of Film: The Redemption of Physical Reality*. London, Oxford, New York: Oxford University Press, 1971.

Law Kar (ed). *Early Images of Hong Kong and China*. Hong Kong: The Urban Council, 1995.

Lee, Leo Ou-fan. *Shanghai Modern: The Flowering of a New Urban Culture in China, 1930–1945*. Cambridge, MA: Harvard University Press, 1999.

Leyda, Jay. *Dianying, Electric Shadows: An Account of Films and the Film Audience in China*. Cambridge, MA: The MIT Press, 1972.

Li Suyuan and Hu Jubin. *Chinese Silent Film History*. Beijing: China Film Press, 1997.

Ling, Pan. *In Search of Old Shanghai*. Hong Kong: Joint Publishing Company, 1983.

Liu, Alan D. L. *Communications and National Integration in Communist China*. Berkeley, Los Angeles: University of California Press, 1971.

Lu, Sheldon Hsiao-peng. *Transnational Chinese Cinemas*. Honolulu: University of Hawaii Press, 1999.

Lu Xun. *Ah Q and Others: Selected Stories of Lu Xun*. New York: Columbia University Press, 1941.

Mao Tun. *Spring Silkworms and Other Stories*. Beijing: Foreign Language Press, 1956.

Marion, Donald J. *The Chinese Filmography*. Jefferson, NC: McFarland, 1997.

Meyer, Richard J. *Ruan Ling-yu: The Goddess of Shanghai*. Hong Kong: Hong Kong University Press, 2005.

Miller, G. E. *Shanghai, The Paradise of Adventurers*. Shanghai: Wong Wei, 1937.

Moise, Edwin E. *Modern China: A History*. London and New York: Longman, 1986.

Mosely, George. *China since 1911*. New York, Evanston: Harper and Row, 1968.

Murowchick, Robert E. *China: Ancient Culture, Modern Land (Cradles of Civilization)*. Norman, OK: University of Oklahoma Press, 1994.

Pang, Laikwan. *Building a New China in Cinema: The Chinese Left-Wing Movement, 1932–1937*. Lanhan, MD: Rowman and Littlefield, 2002.

Phillips, Richard T. *China since 1911*. New York: St. Martin's Press, 1996.

Qin Yi. *I Play All the Roles*. Shanghai: Shanghai Press, 1997.

Rayns, Tony and Meek, Scott (eds). *Electric Shadows: 45 Years of Chinese Cinema*. London: BFI, 1980.

Rummel, R. J. *China's Bloody Century: Genocide and Mass Murder since 1900*. New Brunswick: Transaction Publishers, 1991.

Schoppa, R. Keith. *The Columbia Guide to Modern Chinese History*. New York: Columbia University Press, 2000.

Schwarcz, Vera. *The Chinese Enlightenment: Intellectuals and the Legacy of the May Fourth Movement of 1919*. Berkeley, Los Angeles, London: University of California Press, 1986.

Selected Posters of China's Films (1905–1995). Guangzhou Association for Cultural Exchange with Foreign Countries. Beijing: China Film Archive, Guangzhou Publishing House, 1995.

Selected Works of Lu Xun, Vol. 4. Translated by Yang Hsien-yi and Yang, Gladys. Beijing: Foreign Language Press, 1960.

Sensel, George S., Hong Xia, and Ping Jian (eds). *Chinese Film Theory*. New York: Praeger, 1990.

Sergeant, Harriet. *Shanghai*. London: Jonathan Cape, 1991.

Sheridan, James E. *China in Disintegration: The Republican Era in Chinese History, 1912–1949*. New York: The Free Press/Macmillan, 1975.

Shieh, Milton. *The Kuomintang: Selected Historical Documents, 1894–1969*. New York: St. John's University Press, 1970.

Shih, Shu-mei. *The Lure of the Modern: Writing Modernism in Semicolonial China, 1917–1937*. Berkeley, Los Angeles, London: University of California Press, 2001.

Silbergeld, Jerome. *China into Film: Frames of Reference in Contemporary Chinese Cinema*. London: Reaktion Books, 1999.

Snow, Lois Wheeler. *Edgar Snow's China: A Personal Account of the Chinese Revolution*. New York: Vintage Books, 1983.

Soled, Debra E. (ed). *China: A Nation in Transition*. Washington, D.C.: Congressional Quarterly, 1995.

Spence, Jonathan D. *The Gate of Heavenly Peace: The Chinese and Their Revolution, 1895–1980*. New York: Viking Press, 1981.

Spence, Jonathan D. *The Search for Modern China*. New York and London: W. W. Norton and Company, 1990.

Tam, Kwok-kan and Dissanayake, Wimal. *New Chinese Cinema*. Hong Kong: Oxford University Press, 1998.

Tien, Hung-mao. *Government and Politics in KMT China, 1927–1937*. Stanford: Stanford University Press, 1972.

Thomas, Brian. *VideoHound's Dragon: Asian Action and Cult Flicks*. Detroit: Visible Ink Press, 2003.

Tuchman, Barbara W. *Stillwell and the American Experience in China, 1911–1945*. New York: Grove Press, 1970.

Wakemen, Frederick, Jr. *Policing Shanghai, 1927–1937*. Berkeley, Los Angeles, London: University of California Press, 1995.

Wakemen, Frederick, Jr. and Yeh Wen-Hsin (eds). *Shanghai Sojourners*. Berkeley: Institute of East Asian Studies, University of California, 1992.

Wales, Nym (Helen Foster Snow) and San, Kim. *Song of Ariran: A Korean Communist in the Chinese Revolution*. San Francisco: Ramparts Press, 1941.

Wang, Renmei. *Wo de cheng ming yu bu xing: Wang Renmei hui yi lu*. Shanghai: Shanghai wen yi chu ban she: xin hua shu dian Shanghai fa xing suo fa xing, 1985.

Wang, Y. C. *Chinese Intellectuals and the West, 1872–1949*. Chapel Hill: University of North Carolina Press, 1966.

Wei, Betty Peh-T'i. *Old Shanghai*. Hong Kong: Oxford University Press, 1993.

Wei, Betty Peh-T'i. *Shanghai: Crucible of Modern China*. Hong Kong, Oxford, New York: Oxford University Press, 1987.

Widmer, Ellen and Wang, David Der-wei (eds). *From May Fourth to June Fourth: Fiction and Film in Twentieth-Century China*. Cambridge: Harvard University Press, 1993.

Yang, Jeff. *Once upon a Time in China*. New York: Atria Books, 2003.

Yao, Fang Zao. *Qin Yi: Shen Yuan Zhong De Mingxing*. Shanghai: Shanghai wen yi chu ban she, 1989.

Yeh, Wen-Hsin (ed). *Becoming Chinese: Passages to Modernity and Beyond*. Berkeley, Los Angeles, London: University of California Press, 2000.

Zhang, Yingjin. *Chinese National Cinema*. New York, London: Routledge, 2004.

Zhang, Yingjin (ed). *Cinema and Urban Culture in Shanghai, 1922–1943*. Stanford: Stanford University Press, 1999.

Zhang, Yingjin. *The City in Modern Chinese Literature and Film: Configurations of Space, Time, and Gender*. Stanford, Stanford University Press, 1996.

Zhang, Yingjin and Xiao Zhiwei. *Encyclopedia of Chinese Film.* London and New York: Routledge, 1998.

Zhang, Zhen. *An Amorous History of the Silver Screen: Shanghai Cinema, 1896–1937.* Chicago and London: University of Chicago Press, 2005.

Zhu, Ying. *Chinese Cinema during the Era of Reform: The Ingenuity of the System.* Westport, CN: Praeger, 2003.

Articles and Periodicals

Bergère, Marie-Claire. "'The Other China': Shanghai from 1919 to1949," in Christopher Howe (ed), *Shanghai: Revolution and Development in an Asian Metropolis.* Cambridge: Cambridge University Press, 1981, p. 16.

Berry, Chris. "Films of the Cultural Revolution," *Journal of Asian Culture*, VI: 1982, pp. 37–72.

Braester, Yomi. "A Big Dying Vat," *Modern China*, Vol. 31, No. 4, October 2005, pp. 411–47.

Braester, Yomi. "Chinese Cinema in the Age of Advertisement: The Filmmaker as a Cultural Broker," *The China Quarterly*, September 2005, pp. 549–64.

Braester, Yomi. "From Real Time to Virtual Reality: Chinese Cinema in the Internet Age," *Journal of Contemporary China*, 2004, 13 (38), February, pp. 89–104.

Caesar, Diane. "Chinese Film: Sources and Resources," *Cinema Journal* 34, No. 4, Summer 1995.

Chang, Michael G. "The Good, the Bad, and the Beautiful," in Yingjin Zhang (ed), *Cinema and Urban Culture in Shanghai, 1922–1943.* Stanford: Stanford University Press, 1999, p. 143.

Cheng Jihua, Li Shubai, and Xing Zuwen. "Chinese Cinema: Catalogue of Films, 1905–1937," *Griffithiana*, 54, October 1995, p. 41.

Cho, Pock-rey. "The Emperor of Shanghai Movies of the 1930s, Jin Yan," *Asian Cinema*, 14.2, Fall/Winter, 2003, p. 206.

"Diary of Li Minwei," *Da Zhong Dianying*, August 2003, No. 15, pp. 44–5.

Fu, Poshek. "Between Nationalism and Colonialism: Mainland Émigrés, Marginal Culture, and Hong Kong Cinema, 1937–1941," in Fu and Desser (eds), *The Cinema of Hong Kong: History, Arts, Identity*. Cambridge: Cambridge University Press, 2000, pp. 199–226.

Fu, Poshek. "The Ambiguity of Entertainment: Chinese Cinema in Japanese Occupied Shanghai, 1941 to 1945," *Cinema Journal*, 37, No. 1, Fall 1997, pp. 66–84.

He Ling (Shi Linghe). "Sun Yu: His Life and Films," *Zhonghua Tuhua Zazhi* (China Picture Magazine), No. 45, August 1936, in *Griffithiana*, 60/61, October 1997, pp. 155–61.

Hoffman, Hugh. "Film Conditions in China," *The Moving Picture World*, July 25, 1914, p. 577.

Horowitz, Stephen. "Brief History of the Chinese Cinema," *American Film Institute China Week Brochure*, 1981.

Lee, Leo Ou-fan. "The Cultural Construction of Modernity in Urban Shanghai: Some Preliminary Explorations," in Wen-Hsin Yeh (ed), *Becoming Chinese: Passages to Modernity and Beyond*. Berkeley, Los Angeles, London: University of California Press, 2000, pp. 31–61.

Lee, Leo Ou-fan. "Urban Milieu of Shanghai Cinema," in Yingjin Zhang (ed), *Cinema and Urban Culture in Shanghai, 1922–1943*. Stanford: Stanford University Press, 1999, p. 85.

"Leftist Chinese Cinema of the Thirties," *Cineaste* XVII, No. 3, 1990.

Leyda, Jay. "China Enters the International Film World," *American Film Institute China Week Brochure*, 1981.

Li, H.C. "Chinese Electric Shadows: A Selected Bibliography of Materials in English," *Modern Chinese Literature*, Vol. 7, 1993, pp. 117–53.

Marchetti, Gina. "'Two Stage Sisters': The Blossoming of a Revolutionary Aesthetic," in Sheldon Hsiao-Penglu (ed), *Transnational Chinese Cinema*. Honolulu: University of Hawaii Press, 1997, pp. 59–80.

Patterson, Richard C., Jr. "The Cinema in China," *China Weekly Review* (Shanghai) 40: 48–9, March 12, 1927.

Pickowicz, Paul. "Melodramatic Representation and the 'May Fourth' Tradition of Chinese Cinema," in Ellen Widmer and David Der-wei Wang (eds), *From May Fourth to June Fourth: Fiction and Film in Twentieth-Century China*. Cambridge, MA: Harvard University Press, 1993, pp. 295–326.

Rayns, Tony. "Early Images of Hong Kong and China," in Law Kar (ed), *Early Images of Hong Kong and China*. Hong Kong: The Urban Council, 1995, p. 110.

Schell, Orville. "China — The End of an Era," *The Nation*, July 17–24, 1995, p. 86.

Shih, Joan Chung-wen. "Dominant Themes and Values in Chinese Films," *American Film Institute China Week Brochure*, 1981.

Strand, David. "The City in the Making of Modern China," in Wen-Hsin Yeh (ed), *Becoming Chinese: Passages to Modernity and Beyond*. Berkeley, Los Angeles, London: University of California Press, 2000, pp. 98–136.

"The Chinese Film Industry," *The People's Tribune* IX, April 1, XXIV, 1935, pp. 25–33.

Tiang Xing, "The Minxin Studio and Its New Studio (Qian di wei liang hua Minxin)," *Shadow Play Journal* 1.1 (1929).

Treat, Ida. "China Makes Its Own Movies," *Travel* 67: 32–5, 56–7, June 1936.

Vincent, Jean-Louis. "Life in Peking: Report from a Long Nose," *The NY Times Magazine*, February 26, 1967.

Wei Haoming. "Playboy Swordsman," *New Silver Star (Xin ying xing)* 16 (1929).

Xia Yan. "Remember the Past as a Lesson for the Future," translated by Fong Kenk Ho, *Dianying Yishu*, No. 1, 1979, in Rayns and Meek (eds), *Electric Shadows: 45 Years of Chinese Cinema*. London: BFI, 1980.

Zhang, Zhen. "Teahouse, Shadowplay, Bricolage: Laborer's Love and the Question of Early Chinese Cinema," in Yingjin Zhang (ed), *Cinema and Urban Culture in Shanghai, 1922–1943*. Stanford: Stanford University Press, 1999, p. 36.

Newspapers

Shanghai Star, March 27, 2003.

The International Herald Tribune, January 26, 2006.

The Korea Times, August 15, 2005.

The New York Times, November 8, 1936

The New York Times, June 14, 1942.

The New York Times, November 13, 1944.

The New York Times, April 1, 2007.

Web Sites

The Encyclopedia of World History. http://www.bartleby.com/67/1430.html/

http://www.medicine.yonsei.ac.KR/EN/

Interviews

Jin Fei Heng, December 17, 2005.
John Zao, March 1, 2007.
Qin Yi, December 15, 16, 17, 2005.

Unpublished Works

Clark, Paul. "Chinese Cinema in the Second Half of the Seventies." Paper presented to the Workshop on Contemporary Chinese Literature and the Performing Arts, John King Fairbank Center for East Asian Research. Harvard University, June 12–20, 1979.

Hu, Jubin. "Chinese National Cinema before 1949." Unpublished PhD dissertation, School of Communication, Arts and Critical Enquiry, La Trobe University, Australia, 2001.

Pickowicz, Paul G. and Yu, Nien Ch'Ao. "Political and Ideological Themes in Chinese Films of the Early Sixties: A Review Essay." Workshop on Contemporary Chinese Literature and the Performing Arts, John King Fairbank Center for East Asian Research. Harvard University, June 12–20, 1979.

Other Materials

Choi, Kai-kwong. *Lai Man-wai: Father of Hong Kong Cinema*. DVD. Hong Kong: Dragon Ray Motion Pictures, Ltd., 2001.

The Peach Girl. DVD. San Francisco: San Francisco Silent Film Festival, 2005.

About the Author

R ichard J. Meyer teaches film at Seattle University. He was the Distinguished Research Fellow in the Center for Film, Media and Popular Culture at Arizona State University in 2007 and the Distinguished Fulbright Professor at I'Universita' del Piemonte Orientale Amedeo Avogadro in Italy for the spring 2005 trimester. Dr. Meyer is Edmund F. and Virginia B. Ball Professor of Telecommunications Emeritus at Ball State University in Muncie, Indiana and visiting professor at the Center for Journalism and Media Studies at the University of Hong Kong.

In 2001, he was a Fellow of the Asian Cultural Council in Hong Kong. Prior to his appointment to the endowed chair, he was Fulbright scholar at National Chengchi University in Taiwan where he studied Chinese Silent Films at the Beijing, Taipei, and Hong Kong Film Archives. Dr. Meyer received his BA and MA Degrees from Stanford University and his PhD from New York University. His post-doctoral fellowships were at Columbia University, the East-West Center in Honolulu, and Arizona State University.

While pursuing a career in public broadcasting as a producer and executive with WNET, New York and CEO at KCTS Seattle and KERA/KDTN Dallas, he maintained a passion for film by experimenting with the medium as noted by *TV Guide* in April of 1969. He has been published in *Public Opinion Quarterly*, *Journal of Broadcasting*, *Educational Broadcasting Review*, *Film Comment*, *NEA Journal*, *Time (Asia)* and other periodicals and books. His chapter "Blacks and Broadcasting" appears in the book *Broadcasting and Bargaining* published by the University of Wisconsin Press. His section on "The Films of David Wark Griffith" is featured in *Focus on D.W. Griffith*, published by Prentice-Hall. His piece "Reaction to the 'Blue Book'" is presented in *American Broadcasting* published by Hastings House.

Dr. Meyer has written about the Pordenone International Silent Film Festival for *American Way Magazine*, the *Dallas Morning News* and other publications. In addition, he has produced two CDs, *Piano Themes from the Silent Screen* and *Piano Portraits of the Goddess* and two DVDs, the 1934 classic Chinese film *The Goddess* and the 1931 Shanghai hit *The Peach Girl*. His book, *Ruan Ling-yu: The Goddess of Shanghai*, was published by Hong Kong University Press in 2005.

Throughout the United States, Asia, Southern Africa, and Europe, Dr. Meyer has been a broadcasting consultant, technical and media advisor to public and private schools, cultural groups, the State University of New York, UNESCO, the Corporation for Public Broadcasting, the United States Information Agency, and various radio and television institutions. He has worked in all phases of film and educational television production.

The series "Communications and Education", on which he served as executive producer, won the Ohio State Award in 1968. His film *The Garden of Eden* was responsible, in part, for saving the Garden of Eden in Lucas, Kansas. He has been a speaker at the Buster Keaton Celebration, the Taiwan International Symposium on Public Media, the International Film Studies Conference, the

International Federation of Film Archives (FIAF) Congress, and numerous venues about film and broadcasting.

Dr. Meyer was a member of the President's Communications Council at Howard University, an associate of the Columbia University's seminar on public communications, and an adjunct professor at Simon Fraser University in British Columbia, the University of Texas at Dallas and the University of North Texas. He was a member of the board of directors of the National Association of Educational Broadcasters, the board of managers of the Public Broadcasting Service, the board of directors of the Public Broadcasting Service, and the president of the Washington Educational Network. He served on the Executive Committee of the American Program Service, the Executive Board of the Meadows School of the Arts at Southern Methodist University, and as a member of the National Advisory Council of the Van Cliburn International Piano Competition and a director of the National Museum of Communications.

Presently Dr. Meyer is president emeritus of The San Francisco Silent Film Festival and a member of the Board of Directors of the Seattle International Film Festival. He produces and introduces restored silent films accompanied by music at various "LIVE CINEMA" presentations. He is a certified scuba instructor of the National Association of Underwater Instructors. His underwater photographs and articles about diving have appeared in various magazines.